P9-DXM-638

D0037885

Praise for
Bird Uncaged

"Marlon Peterson lyrically and powerfully narrates his own experience with the injustices of American prisons, from the cruelty of incarceration to the cages of masculinity. *Bird Uncaged* is a freedom dream, and important reading for anyone thinking deeply about our carceral systems."

—Ibram X. Kendi, National Book Award–winning author of *Stamped from the Beginning* and *How to Be an Antiracist*

"Marlon Peterson's memoir tells the intimate story of how the twin forces of patriarchy and white supremacy have combined to build a life of cages for generations of Black men in America. Marlon's work—a narrative of men who have suffered under, been complicit in, and then attempted to upend their involvement in patriarchal systems—is just the kind of book we need to build toward a liberated future for all Black people in America."

—Kimberlé Crenshaw, author of *On Intersectionality*

"Peterson's words are necessary balm. And we need them now more than ever. What a gift he has given us in his debut book."

—Darnell Moore, author of *No Ashes in the Fire*

"Marlon Peterson's gift is one of immense heart. He has been tested throughout his life—he has had his freedom taken away from him in the most real sense. That has provided Marlon with the kind of perspective often missing from conversations of justice and violence and transformation and healing."

—Mychal Denzel Smith, author of *Stakes Is High*

"Peterson has done what is rarely done in American literature: created a classic memoir that shows contemporary readers how to rewrite our lives and future readers how to reread the possibilities of abolition. This is a stunning memoir that pulls off everything it attempts and somehow it made me want to ask more of myself as a writer, human, and abolitionist."

—Kiese Laymon, author of *Heavy*

"*Bird Uncaged* is a story of trauma and survival—a lesson in what it means to confront all of the ugliness of the past and dare journey to forgiveness and something more. Peterson is resolute in these lines, because he has seen enough to know that the healing and the hope is in the journey. The journey found in these pages isn't just a coming-of-age story, but rather is a crucially important [story] confronting the ways a man has hurt and been hurt, and come to believe honesty might be a pathway away from shame and more suffering."

—Reginald Dwayne Betts, author of *Felon*

"*Bird Uncaged* is an exquisitely excruciating exercise in emotional excavation that is at once a profoundly personal story as well as a sweeping indictment of this country's systems and norms and practices. Bravo, Marlon. I am grateful for your intrepidity, voice, and humanity."

—Sophia Chang, author of *The Baddest Bitch in the Room*

"In *Bird Uncaged*, Marlon Peterson offers compelling insights from his remarkable life story. It is a tale for our times: how a young man of promise ends up finding meaning and direction despite numerous challenges and obstacles, not least of which is a lengthy stint in prison. Bracingly powerful and painfully honest, *Bird Uncaged* is a call for change that should be read by anyone with an interest in justice in the United States."

—Greg Berman, executive director of the
Center for Court Innovation

"Marlon Peterson's *Bird Uncaged: An Abolitionist's Freedom Song* is a viscerally honest, bracingly insightful, exquisitely lyrical memoir that is impossible to put down and even more impossible to ever forget having read. It is raw testimony. It bears witness to modern-day slavery. And it is a full-on education about what America is and what it foolishly imagines itself to be. The book should be required reading in schools from one end of the USA to another."

—Dr. Baz Dreisinger, author of *Incarceration Nations*

"*Bird Uncaged* is heart-wrenching without being sentimental. It's beautiful without ever being flowery. It's one voice without ever being just one thing. It's all honest without ever pretending to be complete. I hope you love it. It deserves to be a thing you love."

—Danielle Sered, author of *Until We Reckon:
Violence, Mass Incarceration, and a Road to Repair*

AN ABOLITIONIST'S FREEDOM SONG

MARLON PETERSON

 BOLD TYPE BOOKS

New York

Bold Type Books
116 East 16th Street, 8th Floor New York, NY 10003
www.boldtypebooks.org
@BoldTypeBooks

Printed in the United States of America

First Edition: April 2021

Published by Bold Type Books, an imprint of Perseus Books, LLC, a subsidiary of Hachette Book Group, Inc. Bold Type Books is a co-publishing venture of the Type Media Center and Perseus Books.

The Hachette Speakers Bureau provides a wide range of authors for speaking events. To find out more, go to www.hachettespeakersbureau.com or call (866) 376-6591.

The publisher is not responsible for websites (or their content) that are not owned by the publisher.

Print book interior design by Amy Quinn.

Library of Congress Control Number: 2020952599

ISBNs: 978-1-64503-651-7 (hardcover), 978-1-64503-650-0 (e-book)

LSC-C

Printing 1, 2021

for the hurt people, and the people who hurt people:
"sit down in this circle"
—Rumi, "A Community of the Spirit"

To Dr. Angelou,
"because your legacy is every **life you touch**."

I don't believe in cages of any kind. Let me tell you why.

CONTENTS

HIDING

Dear Marlo',

The first thing you should know is that you were a beautiful, brilliant, bubbly Black boy. Your big black lips were just the right size. No need to hide them by folding them inwards. No need to hide your presence.

You were talkative, and that was okay. It was your way of sharing your light. No need to hide your voice by playing small. Your smile...your smile was contagious. No need to hide it by masking it with screwfaces. Your ability to carry on big people conversations as an eight-year-old was a gift. No need to hide your maturity. It was one of the ways you learned about the world, even if you did raise your parents' phone bill to over $1,000 dollars by calling 1-900 numbers to play Jeopardy!

You were a nerd. No need to hide your intelligence.

You should know that your 1980s Crown Heights, Brooklyn, neighborhood needed young Black boys like you to shine and inspire.

Too many of you hid, in cages of your own creation, but mostly in cages created for you. Often the two were indistinguishable.

My mother, Elsa, is a hardworking woman who loves her children. She was once a little Black girl in Trinidad who grew up in the 1940s and 1950s. She lived during a time when tightly coiled hair on a girl was considered nigger naps, something to be ashamed of and hide away. So my mom hid her hair under berets to avoid feeling that she was ugly because of her hair. My mom also witnessed both her biological father and her stepfather plagued by alcoholism, and her mom get beaten regularly by the latter. She told me and my pops about the abuse a handful of years ago. She kept that information hidden for over sixty years from two of the closest men in her life. Despite that part of her childhood, Mommy was the gem of her mother's eyes, and spoiled.

Daddy, also known as Jaego but whose government name is Michael, was saga boy, barber, and panman. Saga boy is Trini for a man who is always in fashion who has it good with the chicks. My father was also a steelpan player back when only thugs and poor people were associated with the instrument. His band, North Stars, won the first two National Panorama competitions in Trinidad and he toured the Caribbean with his neighborhood band, Westside Symphony. I am told he was nice with the blades as a barber back in the '60s in Trinidad, but as his son who got Daddy haircuts until my freshman year of high school, I beg to differ.

Daddy grew up living between his biracial grandmother, his father, and his mother. The second oldest of seven, he learned how to survive with few resources since neither of his parents had much of anything. His first exposure to Jehovah's Witnesses came through this grandmother, a Kittitian. His father was also a drunk, but a cool one, I am told. I never met either of my grandfathers—they both died during my infancy—so it's the stories of my parents and older brother and sister that taught me about my grandfathers, romanticized but sprinkled with some real.

Michael and Elsa, both from the same St. James neighborhood in Trinidad, met each other at eighteen and never looked back. They both bought the Kool-Aid of the American dream, though my pops admits today that he read and heard about all the racism in America before he left Trini, but that he convinced himself that none of that racism was happening in New York. It was the South he thought Black people had to fear in America. He was wrong.

I saw the American television and I was attracted to the nice clothes, the parties, and the music. I wanted to try my hand at it. I saw the stories of racism in America, but I didn't realize how serious it was until I get here. They killed Martin Luther King right after I got here. That was real sad.

Elsa was the first of the two to go to New York. She visited in 1965, a few months after Malcolm X was assassinated. She had a friend who lived in Harlem and frequented the Apollo often. But she was severely homesick; she was unaccustomed to the busy-ness of the city, and frightened by the droves of heroin-addicted women and men who languished along the streets of Harlem. After only eight months she retreated back to Trinidad to her mom and her boyfriend, Jaego.

When Jaego had saved enough money to travel to the US, he packed what few belongings he had and decided he would create a new life for himself in America. Elsa joined him. In 1967 they both officially made Brooklyn home—a one-room apartment in Bushwick with a shared bathroom and kitchenette. That was their exposure to the American dream.

One year later they gave birth to my sister, Kelly, who we called Kels, and three years after that, my brother, Mike.

Both of my parents overstayed their visas and lived as undocumented residents of NYC raising two young children with little money and agency. When they found a cigarette burn on Kels after they picked her up from the babysitter, they told no one. They didn't call the police because they feared doing so would mean immigration finding them out, which would lead to deportation. So they figured the best way to deal with the situation would be to pull Kels out of that day care and not allow Mike to go through anything similar.

They decided to send infant Mikey to Trinidad to live with his maternal grandparents. Mike stayed in Trini until 1976, when he was five years old. I think those five years away from our parents caused family drama that no parenting class could prepare my parents for. They didn't have cell phones or computers to communicate with someone living in another country. Airmail letters and expensive long distance calls were their only way of getting in touch. So for the first couple of years of Mike's life, he saw his grandparents as his parents. Of course, he knew of his real parents, but they were foreign to him in a foreign country. Kels would sometimes visit him during the summer months, so he knew his sister. But that could not curtail his feeling that his parents did not love him as much as Kels did.

Mommy and Daddy could have joined Kels to visit Mike, but because of immigration policy, it would have prohibited them from ever returning to the US. Two years earlier the Immigration and Naturalization Act of 1965 had abolished the American immigration quota system that gave preference to Western European immigrants, and excluded everyone else.[1] Prior to the Immigration and Naturalization Act of 1965, American immigration policy gave preference to Western Europeans over Eastern Europeans—classic white on white violence executed through policy. In a speech to the American Committee on Italian Migration in 1963, President Kennedy described these quotas as "nearly intolerable."[2] The 1965 Act, signed by President Lyndon Johnson, opened up American borders to Eastern Europeans, and to *others*. My parents were among the others. Visitor's visas, the golden key that unlocked entry into the US, had expiration dates. If you overstayed the expiration date on that visa, you became civically illegal—an illegal immigrant, illegal alien—though I prefer the term *undocumented resident*.

This ain't just an argument about semantics, though. Since the 1970s, the consequence of being caught overstaying a visa could mean deportation by the US government. So my parents avoided interactions with police, welfare agencies, and other parts of the US government that could expose them as undocumented. They were hiding within cages of their own making, with the help of borders that, though they had finally opened to Black and Brown immigrants, limited the number to twenty thousand per year, exactly. Poor working-class immigrant families like mine made difficult decisions in order to avoid being labeled and deported by the government. My parents overstayed their visitor's visas, becoming the new nigger to America: illegal aliens. They sacrificed their Trinidadian discomfort for a new American discomfort that caged them through policy. Today, if they were to get caught, they'd be put in physical prisons built on old immigration policy. Survival isn't always logical to the observer.

When Mike returned to NY he spoke little to his parents and cried for his grandparents. He was now a foreigner in his parents' home.

And then I was born a few years later in 1979. I was supposed to be an abortion because my parents could barely afford me. Kels told me this years later when I was in my twenties in a cell, though I never felt like a mistake to anyone...except to my brother. We grew up estranged.

My first bed was a beautifully decorated dresser drawer, the penthouse of the dresser set. The other compartments of the dresser were filled to occupancy with clothes and bedding sheets. My parents couldn't immediately afford a crib or bassinet, and though momentary, it would not be the last time I slept in something not made for humans.

Fortunately, one of my father's new Jehovah's Witness friends was told about my sleeping situation and bought me a crib. Another sister from my father's congregation in the Kingdom Hall volunteered to babysit me. Daddy was convinced that Jehovah was blessing him and his family. New job, new baby, and new friends freely giving their time and money to us.

My mother didn't care for it. She had married a man who hung out too often, smoked cigarettes regularly, weed sparingly, and sexed other women discreetly. My mother was content with the man her husband was becoming, but she wanted no part of the religion. She was a baby-baptized Catholic, and though she could tally the number of times she'd been to a church since moving to America on the back of one of our many apartment roaches, she felt she was losing her friend.

With the new godly blessings came rules. Lots of rules. No Christmas or birthday celebrations. No holiday specials on television. Daddy chastised Mommy for using profanity. He viewed soca music as vile and un-Christian.

Mommy cussed, bought us gifts for Christmas, partied, and played her soca music in the house, sometimes behind his back, sometimes in his face. The latter came with arguments, plenty of them.

Mommy was convinced that Daddy was brainwashed into a religious cult. She was incensed that he dragged her three children along with him to the Kingdom Hall.

Michael, alyuh JeeHovah Wickedness ain't nuttin' but ah cult!
Elsa, why yuh ain't hush yuh shtupid mout!

To Mommy, Daddy's sanctimonious evolution was depriving her kids of their childhood. There was a one-hour Bible Study on Tuesdays at 7 p.m., a two-hour service on Wednesday from 7:30 p.m. to 9:30 p.m., field ministry on Saturday mornings for at least two hours, followed by more field ministry on Sunday morning, followed by another two-hour service. Too much religion.

Kels and Mikey were in their early tweens during Daddy's early transition to Brother Peterson, the Jehovah's Witness. His grip on them wasn't as tight; they rebelled against the routinized religiosity. They stopped going a few years after I was born, and Mommy was their excuse. She defended them against Daddy's new blessing, and won.

But me, I was born into the routine. Daddy enrolled me into a Jehovah's Witness preschool, and I loved it. But, when that one year of Jehovah Witness kindergarten ended, I was off to public school—the notorious, at the time, PS 138.

It was here that I first learned to keep hurtful experiences secret.

I was in the first grade the first time I was jumped. I can't remember why they did it, probably because they banged my head so hard, but two classmates slammed my head against the porcelain sink in the boys' bathroom of PS 138. We were probably just playing too rough, at my expense. Dizzy, I struggled to my feet, peed, flushed the toilet, washed my hands, dried my fingers on my clothes, went back to class, sat in my seat, said nothing. I told a silent lie to myself that what had happened to me was too embarrassing to divulge to anyone. I eventually forgot it ever happened, only remembering it during therapy almost three decades later.

Most of the kids in the de facto orphanage of our Brooklyn neighborhood were trying to break free from the lie that we were tasked to work extra hard not to die. Once I stepped outside apartment 4B at 616 Nostrand Avenue I had to navigate other hurting Black boys who were willing to rob and beat me, and intimidate me with stares; I needed to decipher between a harmless crackhead and one who was delusional enough to prey on me for a high. This and more happened before I got to the school where, in the third grade, I witnessed my first face slashing. A couple of rooms away from my third grade classroom a fourth grader was rushed out of class because he was cut on his face by another kid. I don't know why it happened. We saw the kid get carried to the stairwell by nurses and security guards, blood leaking along the way, and we went back to class. No counseling. No nothing. We moved on.

Most of us learned to hide just enough to not be discovered. Discovery could expose you to deportation, drug misuse, AIDS, teen pregnancy, or being killed by police, a crackhead, or some hurting kid from the block. Back in the 1980s, mass incarceration was not a term we knew. We knew that people went to jail, but we had not realized that millions were going to jail, some never to come back home. So our parents were not acutely aware of the Black fear of prison, and neither was I. Black people in prison was more of an abstract idea, something that happened to drug dealers; I didn't yet understand it as the day-to-day weight that we now know always existed for all Black people, just in different outfits. Twist locks evolved into handcuffs. Ankle bracelets are trending now.

The intersection of Nostrand Ave and Pacific Street, or NA Rock as some might know it, was our thoroughfare. We had a doctor's office, pharmacy, a record shop, Chinese takeout, West Indian ital stores, barbershops, a laundromat, a Korean vegetable stand, a hardware store, a Yemeni bodega on one corner, and a Latino-owned bodega on the next end—and that was just my block.

We were poor*ish*, but not in the way that I ever missed a meal. My parents' pride prevented them from admitting to being poor "like dem American Blacks who doh take advantage of all de tings dem have here. We doh have all these opportunities back home." My parents prided themselves on never going on welfare or food stamps because it allowed us to maintain a self-image that othered the welfare and food stamp–dependent people who lived in our drug-infested building. I guess that was their understanding of loving parenting—denying that we were struggling to make ends meet all the time. We were a family of *working* poor, and that difference gave us enough latitude to avoid being labeled as welfare-dependent. Being undocumented was enough. To be dependent on government aid would incur more interactions with the people who could figure out my parents had overstayed their visas, and get them kicked out of the country.

My parents, like most poor Black immigrants in America, created fantastical delusions for the overreach of systemic oppression. "The man" had to be avoided at all costs.

Though we lived in a one-bedroom apartment on the third floor, our apartment was 4B. Nope, that doesn't make sense, and not much on that thoroughfare on Nostrand Ave made sense to me...then. Empty crack vials were everywhere: in our apartment building, floor, elevator, and sidewalks. They were never in piles, but usually in single lines along the edges of the concrete and ornamented with the perfume of piss or a hock spit dressing.

One night, when I was about six or seven, I remember my fidgety mother being more nervous than usual. Kels and Mikey were going in and out of the apartment, and my pops was trying to get everyone to calm down and "mind they bizness," in his fake Black American accent. I was confused, initially, when Mommy told me that our neighbor's teenage daughter had been thrown off the roof of our six-story building. In an attempt to rape her, a man coaxed her upstairs to the roof. The roof door was always broken open. Fighting him off, she was thrown from the roof. She suffered only a broken leg and badly bruised arm and back.

She eventually healed, at least physically, I think. Who knew? I never asked her, nor was I aware that there was more than one way to suffer from pain. Her cast was tagged up with the names of all her friends, and she eventually walked regular. She was good. She moved on.

I was good. We moved on. Another neighbor was killed two floors up from us. We were good. We moved on. An older teen was shot in the head while talking on a pay phone on the corner of Nostrand and Pacific, a clear view from our living room window. Too bad for him and his family, but we were good. We moved on. Gunshots rang from the street often. As long as we followed the protocols we were taught—"take off de lights, get low to de ground, and stay away from that blasted window!"—we could continue watching television without interruption. We were good. We moved on.

I wish someone told me that simply moving on was not freedom from the harm felt and seen. I wonder if anyone taught my parents this lesson.

My father read to me on most nights, even on the nights that gunshots rang out, from a Jehovah's Witness book called *My Book of Bible Stories*. Every two-page story in that book covered an important event in the Bible. From Eve's first sin of listening to the serpent in the book of Genesis to the utopian hope of living forever in a paradise Earth after God and Jesus killed all the wicked people in Armageddon, or God's war. I could not get enough of the stories. By the age of four I was reading the stories along with my father. I began believing the stories. I got mad at Eve for *causing men to sin*. This is when I learned to fear God and give him glory. No glory for me. It was during this time that I developed a love for learning. There was so much to learn about the Bible, and that trickled into my schooling. My interests were piqued during history and language arts class—that is, as long as it did not conflict with anything I learned from the Bible.

I gave my first five-minute speech in front of my congregation when I was eight years old. I was what was called an unbaptized publisher, which meant that I was spiritually qualified to participate in field ministry, conduct Bible studies with people I met in the community, and give five-minute Bible-based talks. My father was proud of a son who was following him, unlike his other children. My mom was proud that her son was mannerly and smart. My siblings did not care for either. The neighborhood thought I was a punk. I thought Jehovah was blessing me.

Daddy was my closest friend during those days. He and I shared a bond that he wished he could experience with Mommy, Mikey, and Kels. When he took me to the park I'd be on the swings while he studied from his *Watchtower* magazine. He taught me how to ride a bike, no training wheels. He affectionately called me *Marlo Barlo*. He made soggy rice with cut sweet corn from the can for me. He made big uneven pancakes. He made french fries for me. We talked about the Bible. We prayed together.

He taught me about the birds and the bees, but not about relationships. He exposed me to Broadway shows and Star Wars, but concealed the story of the steelpan, the instrument he loved as a young man. He inculcated honesty to Jehovah, but left out the part about being honest to myself. He was being a good dad. I loved him because he was a great dad to me. I did not know about his past days as Jaego, the philanderer, cigarette smoker, and weed puffer. I did not know that those parts of him could rub off on me despite his hiding them. I knew that I adored him. Worshipped him. And loved Jehovah. I was dedicated to preaching in the field ministry. At the same time, I wanted to learn more about the world he vigorously tried to tuck away.

CHAPTER TWO

MOVE ON

Dear Marlo,

When I think back to your childhood, you were real good at suicide. The schoolyard game played at PS 138, the elementary school a few yards away from where police killed Arthur Miller.[1] A remixed version of flys up where one kid would bounce a handball high up against a wall while a group of kids vied to catch the descending ball. Remember, if you dropped the ball trying to catch it you had to sprint to the same wall that it bounced off of and yell "suicide!" when you touched it.

If one of the other players picked up the dropped ball before you got to the wall, they had the right to sling the ball at you like a major league baseball pitcher. Some guys would run up to you and sling the ball at your face, back of the neck, and ears. You all played that game in the heat of summer and in the icy winter. There were times that you were hit so hard with a half-frozen handball that you thought your face had split into uneven parts. Although you wanted to cry from the pain sometimes, you understood that crying in public was out of the question, an abomination, considered cowardly even for a seven- or eight-year-old; fighting was a more honorable pain reliever.

We yelled "suicide" to be saved from hurt.

Despite the pain, you loved suicide, partly because you were always good at catching. But the real thrill came from hitting someone with the ball or the danger of being hit. Even back then you were developing the ability to endure and inflict harm.

Suicide was dangerous. There were black eyes, bloody noses, swollen temples, and busted lips. Remember that girl who got hit so hard she passed out—and she wasn't even playing? Someone misfired and thought nothing of it. You thought nothing of it. You kept playing. Maybe it was you who misfired and hit that girl. I wish you had been more attuned to the pain of Black girls at the expense of your own fun, or trauma, or inclination to hide. I wish I was more attuned in my adult years.

Life for us was similar to that game eerily called suicide. The slightest mistake usually resulted in the most severe pain. That hurt was before Biggie Smalls penned the articulable language "do or die." Before then most of us were just doing and trying not to die, but without the syntax. Just like the game of suicide, you could not choose where you would be hit, just be ready to feel pain. Similarly, life did not give me the choice of consequences, I just had to be ready for the next bad thing to happen. This is the story that you will have to fight to not believe. These are the stories that I want to break free from; the stories I don't want to arrest you. Don't be paroled by these experiences. Create a liberation from a world that embeds within us our own overseer, slaver, jailer, parole officer, and undertaker. Try not to let your pain lead you. At some point I want you to understand that everyone and everything that scarred you was not your fault.

Sixth grade was a tough year for me. Sixth grade was a successful school year for me.

Back in 1990, IS 390 in Crown Heights was an infamous junior high school. It was across the street from Albany Houses, a nine-building high-rise residential experiment for poor Black and Brown people. Elevators never worked, building maintenance budgets were not prioritized, and people were left to act like owners of a building where the landlord was the City of New York. This was the projects and the people living there were taken care of like a project no one cared about.

Like all other geographies that surround housing projects, people did dumb unloving shit. Cursed teachers out in school. Organized themselves into gangs. Robbed each other. Shot each other. There were 2,605 murders and 112,380 reported robberies in NYC that year, the highest ever. A lot of unnecessarily dumb and harmful things were happening in 1990, and not just in New York City. Black unemployment was three times that of whites. Brooklyn had the highest number of HIV/AIDS cases in the city, and 50 percent of those people were Black. *Forty-five percent* of Black women who headed households in the country were poor. The media, police, and politicians told us that crack was a Black drug, though crack-cocaine was really a poor white drug, with over 65 percent of whites admitting they used to pipe up— compared to 26 percent of Blacks. That's not my stat. That's the

United States Sentencing Commission Report to Congress. Some of us bought into the narrative that white life was better. We shot, robbed, raped, and harmed our own communities in the ways we were conditioned to by media, police, and politicians—as illegal aliens, crackheads, crack babies, lazy welfare queens, predators, and promiscuous STD carriers. But there were always reasons behind our so-called senseless violence—our monstrous acts. Who taught us that there was no sense behind our responses to being treated senseless and unempathetically? Survival of the oppressed isn't always logical to the oppressor when observing the oppressed. None of our people are monsters—none. The moment we describe people as monsters we shift human behavior into the realm of the unexplainable. Every act of violence can be explained—especially ghetto shit.

Remember, running away from slavery was a crime and a diagnosis for mental illness. Senseless running away. Yet, entire biographies get written when white boys and white men shoot up concerts, churches, synagogues, schools, and protestors. White people made us believe that our pain was monstrous, senseless, and pathological. We have reasons.[2]

Anyways, I only lasted a month or two in IS 390. It was the first time I would be robbed. My victimization wasn't reported to the police, so I wasn't included in that 1990 statistic of 112,380 robberies.

It was early in the new school year. I started the sixth grade at ten years old and it was the first time I was in a school where we went to different classrooms from period to period. One day me and a couple of my new classmates were going down the steps to lunch. There were several separate but adjacent stairwells leading to the lunchroom. I decided to take a separate stairwell from my classmates. I always had a penchant for taking my own course.

A few steps into the three or four flight rush down to the lunchroom three gigantic eighth graders approached me in the stairwell, patted my pockets stop-and-frisk style (like the police modeled for us), and took all of my belongings—this time fifty-five cents and a half-fare bus pass. I didn't fight back or yell. I didn't know how to react. I had heard about other kids getting robbed on their way to or from school, but never in a way that I had interpreted that it really bothered them. I wanted to keep it a secret. I didn't want anyone to think I was a punk. Even ten-year-old boys gotta hold their masculinity intact. I hid the hurt.

A classmate who had witnessed everything went and told a teacher, who then told the dean of the sixth grade. Why didn't he jump in and help me instead of watching, I wondered.

The dean, a legally blind middle-aged Black man, fetched me from the lunchroom. He paraded me around the entire school hoping I would point out the culprits. Even at ten I knew that this was the worst thing he could do. If I pointed out the kids who had robbed me, they or their friends would come after me for snitching.

Yo, Marlon! Big Mike is your big brother, right? Tell that nigga. He gone find them niggas for you! Fuck that blind-ass nigga!

An unfamiliar boy's voice shouted that out from the stairwell as I was on my parade; police call this a show up. I never saw the person who said it. I didn't know that word of the robbery had made its way around the school. I didn't know that people in IS

390 knew my brother. I didn't know that people knew Mikey and I were brothers. I didn't think Mikey would care about anything that happened to me.

I tried to keep it quiet by not telling my parents or siblings that I was robbed at school. But the dean still called my mom later that evening to tell her what had happened to me. I felt like a bigger punk because as soon as Mommy got off the phone with the dean she announced, "Marlon, yuh not going back to that school again. I will find ah next school to put you in."

I hated my mother for that decision. I needed to go back to the school and show that I wasn't scared, that I could survive IS 390. I needed to prove my manhood. I was terrified, actually, but I knew fear wouldn't make things better.

I never attended IS 390 again. I moved on. Fear won.

For years after that incident I would hear kids in my neighborhood repeating that robbery story.

Marlon got robbed and never came back to school.

Hearing ten- and eleven-year-old boys and girls call you a punk was worse than actually being beat up. Add in the fact that I was Jehovah's Witness and I had become the punchline of jokes. The school I was transferred to, PS 138, my old school, was tough for me, too. I fought often because of class bullies like Duke, and other school bullies from the Nostrand Avenue stretch in Crown Heights.

I was bullied because I had big lips, or because some kid saw me over the weekend with a suit and tie "asking for money" by selling *Watchtower* and *Awake!* magazines, or because I was too quiet, or because kids knew I was robbed in IS 390, or because I walked lazily like I was gay.

At this time in my life the Kingdom Hall was one of the only places I could feel safe from the ridicule. No one made fun of me there...well, not to the point of it feeling unsafe. The other kids there still made fun of my big lips, but it didn't hurt as much as it did when I was at school, or when my older brother or sister made a lippopotamus joke.

My Tuesday and Wednesday evenings were spent at the Kingdom Hall. Basically, any time I was not in school I was involved with something around my religion—the religion of my father. Because Jehovah's Witnesses believed that association with worldly people should be limited, after-school programs, school athletic teams, and summer camps were off-limits for me. Daddy was strict when it came to religion, and he did all he could to ensure that his youngest child would be raised according to his religion, whether my mother liked it or not.

It almost worked.

As the head of the household, Daddy succeeded in keeping his family together in the same house, but not as Jehovah's Witnesses. He failed at helping Mike and I develop a brotherly bond. I grew up hating Mike, and I didn't think he cared much what I thought about him. Which is why when Kelly gave birth to my nephew, Devon, who we called DJ, in 1988, I prayed to God that I would be the big brother to him that I never had. I didn't think about what a little brother could mean to his older sibling. Years later, DJ would become the person who gave me life when I wanted to die.

Another good thing at the time were my friends in the Kingdom Hall. Jay and Zoop were my two closest friends there. Jay's parents and Zoop's were both in the truth. Their fathers had cars. They were close to their older sisters. They both made fun of how big my lips were, but at least they liked being around me. Mike made fun of my big lips, too, but that was the substance of our relationship. I looked forward to every Tuesday, Wednesday, and Sunday service at the Kingdom Hall. Those were the times I'd get to see my real brothers. As we grew older, we smoked our first weed together, drank our first St. Ides together, went to our first house party together, and held guns together, all before the age of fifteen.

Even though I was still going to Kingdom Hall three times a week, I had changed that year. I had left IS 390 a lot less innocent. Getting robbed instilled a fear in me that other kids could sense in my new/old school. PS 138's reputation wasn't much better than IS 390's, but it was the only school in my zone that I could transfer to in the middle of the school year.

The story of my robbery had gotten to PS 138, and kids felt that they could antagonize me about it—daily. In years past, when kids got under my skin, I'd fight without thinking, but that robbery of my fifty-five cents also burglarized my sense that I could defend myself. My class bully, Duke, made fun of me and pounced on me every moment the teacher turned her back. Fifth graders from the class next door pounced on that fear. Whenever I was in earshot of them in the schoolyard or the hallways, they'd say things to their friends like, "Yo, that nigga mad pussy, son!"

And, I believed I was pussy. I let myself get robbed. That was the story I told myself, that I believed.

I remember being chased home by two of those fifth graders. When I got home, breathing heavily, and just happy I could hide in my apartment, I told no one why I was breathing heavily. My parents were at work, and my sister and brother weren't home from high school yet, so there was no one to ask me what was wrong.

I moved on.

I went to the Kingdom Hall and sought the religion as a place of peace. In prayer I asked Jehovah to protect me. I asked him to bless me. Jehovah was too busy to listen to me most of the time.

Near the end of the school year, Duke kicked me in my back as we were lining up to go to the auditorium for graduation practice, and I flipped. I turned around, picked up a chair, and hit him with it. He fell to the floor. The teacher broke it up before he could recover. My father was called to the school, and I felt a measure of justice. No one was punished. Duke didn't bother me again for the rest of the school year. But I never became free of the fear of being bothered or beaten again by him or anyone else.

Several weeks later, I was chosen to be the valedictorian of my sixth grade graduating class. I moved on.

Daddy bought a new camera for the occasion, but he didn't know how to use it right, so none of the pictures developed. Sometimes mistakes matter more than they actually should. Sometimes missed memories matter more than we can ever grasp. All I know is that being a valedictorian felt insignificant until I was in a courtroom years later seeking to be seen as someone more significant than the mistake I'd made; and more than a bad memory in the minds of innocent people I'd harmed.

The whole school auditorium of PS 138, including the balcony, was filled. Some kids wore new sneakers, some baggy suits, some in clothes they wore to school every day, some in their one funeral outfit. We were all there and so were older people of all sorts: parents and aunties, uncles, grammies, ma's, Thanias, Ians, and loads of siblings and play cousins. They were all there.

Black families always came out for graduations. We love celebrating.

It was the biggest group of people I had spoken to. By then I was regularly giving five-minute Bible-based talks at the Kingdom Hall, but that was at most seventy, occasionally ninety people. They called those group meetings the Theocratic Ministry School. It was a public speaking course for the Bible. This was where I learned skills like voice modulation, using eye contact and gestures, and the good use of examples.

My father researched and wrote my first two talks, but after that he said I had to do it myself. He would let me practice the delivery of the talk with him, but he wasn't doing any of the researching or writing. He had his own talks to prepare. He was also teaching me a lesson: "Marlo, if you want to learn something you have to find it for yourself."

I thought he was being difficult and lazy and I was hardheaded so I never understood his lessons while in class. After I was pissed off with him for making me do the work, I'd finally get around to doing the researching and writing.

Kelly, though, wrote most, or maybe all, of my valedictorian speech. I had never given a speech about anything outside the Bible, so I asked her to help. As an elementary school valedictorian I said high school–type words to ten-year-olds, got a $100 savings bond, and was accepted into a gifted and talented junior high public school named Satellite East in Bed-Stuy. The school was a few blocks from where Biggie Smalls sold crack, likely during the same time, too. He wasn't seen as fully human by most white people yet, nor was his neighborhood, or the gifted and talented skills that we brought. Still, Satellite East was where I was exposed to my gift for writing.

My seventh grade homeroom and English teacher, Mr. Levine, a Jewish guy who looked like a mix between the basketball coach P. J. Carlesimo and the dude who painted on PBS, pulled me to the side after class, complimented my writing, and asked me to write for the school newspaper. I took the offer. It was the first time I saw my writing as something. I remember writing a piece about not being a statistic when it comes to STDs. I knew nothing about sex, but I knew you didn't want to get AIDS and girls didn't want to get pregnant. I was a published writer and that's all that really mattered to me.

Mr. Levine got me into a summer writing program for the *Fort Greene News* that Spike Lee and Nike sponsored, so I spent the summer of 1992 writing for a community newspaper.

Some days they took us out to notable places in the neighborhood to conjure up story ideas for the newspaper. One time they took us to jail to meet with a panel of incarcerated men so they could tell us about their experiences in jail. I remember a guy saying he once saw someone get stabbed because they were staring at someone else. That's all I remember about my first trip to jail.

So, yeah, a male version of Michelle Pfeiffer in *Dangerous Minds* exposed me to the idea of writing as vocation. He was great at his job, and I appreciate him for it.

During the next two years of school my family moved to a new block with a notorious reputation in Crown Heights, St. Marks Avenue. I was robbed two more times on my way home from school, once for a Tampa Bay Buccaneers Starter cap, and another time for my JanSport book bag. Both times it happened a block away from school. Both times by older boys. Both times I was by myself. Both times I was too scared to fight back. Both times I told no one.

I prayed to Jehovah to protect me. I studied the Bible harder.

The Crown Heights riots happened. The Rodney King beating happened.

I moved on.

Our new home was a two-bedroom apartment. I shared a room with Mikey, Kels, and DJ. Our new apartment building was closer to the Kingdom Hall I attended. It was also a building and block that had lots of kids my age, which meant lots of kids who I had to prove myself to, while making sense of how those police officers who beat Rodney King senseless in Los Angeles could be found not guilty. And how was it that those Jewish people who also lived in Crown Heights and owned both buildings I lived in, evicting us from the first building, could get away with running over and killing a little boy from Guyana. That killing sparked the 1991 Crown Heights riots where the Hasidic Jewish community squared off with the Black side of the neighborhood. Decades of reluctant tolerance between the very different cultures became irritated, tensions grew, and finally the neighborhood exploded.

Thankfully, it was during this time that I met Kofi. Shorter than me, Kofi and I had lots of things in common. He was my age, a child of Trinidadian parents, excelled in school, and was a little nerdy like me.

The one problem, a major one, was that he wasn't a Jehovah's Witness. His parents had long dreadlocks, and his father openly smoked weed—all red flags for my Jehovah's Witness conscience and antithetical to who my father wanted me being around. They were worldly, which meant that they did not follow Jehovah.

But they still felt safe to me. Zoop and Jay, my friends from the Kingdom Hall, lived in Bed-Stuy. Kofi lived in my building. Kofi loved soca and reggae like me. My Jehovah's Witness friends couldn't relate. Our bond was our religious beliefs back then, and

I was feeling less connected to the religion because, well, Jehovah was being too busy to listen to me. He wasn't protecting me.

Kofi and I first connected because we were studying for the New York City specialized high school test; at the time, you could get accepted to one of the top three high schools in NYC—Bronx High School of Science, Brooklyn Technical, and Stuyvesant—if you passed the test. Most Black kids who passed did good enough to get into Brooklyn Tech. The others, Bronx Science and Stuyvesant were mainstays for white kids. But, that was regular to us. It didn't feel abnormal that Black kids had their good schools and white kids had their better schools. I guess what you know can't hurt you, right? We sensed we were worth less than white students, but we didn't grasp the magnitude of that sensation. Years later, the *New York Times* came out with an article that racial discrimination was embedded into the selection process.[3] Racism is always working, ain't it; even when you don't have the data and language to articulate it.

Anyways, though we'd both fail the test by a few points, our friendship turned into a brotherhood for a period of time. If you saw Kofi, you saw me. We went to the store together. Sometimes slept in the same bed. Eventually, we smoked weed, drank brown liquor and Cisco, catcalled girls, and handled guns together. We played steelpan. We worked the same odd jobs and sold a couple of bags of weed during the summer. We did dance routines at neighborhood dancehall reggae house parties—when his mom let him out. He was my brother, and I was his friend. His family was my family, and I was their neighbor.

As close as we were, I didn't tell him about the time I was jumped and robbed during my freshman year of high school. Several boys approached me and two classmates in the empty hallways of George Westinghouse High School. After they patted the pockets of my two cohorts, who ran away before the bullies got to me, the three older boys punched me to the floor after a weak attempt by me to defend myself. Once I was on the floor, they punched and kicked me into a fetal position. I wish I did a better job of blocking my head because they kicked my temples so hard that one of them got swollen. Once again, my mother had to take me out of school because I was too pussy to not get robbed. This time it was only for a couple of weeks, but those weeks being home was enough for me to determine that Jehovah was being derelict in his duties to protect me.

Just like at IS 390 three years earlier, a staff member walked me around the school looking for the boys who beat the shit out of me for nothing, because I had no money for them to take. The boys seemed closer to young men because they looked so much older than me. I later found out that they didn't attend the school but had snuck in to rob pussy little kids like me.

The one bright spot about this incident was that after my mother found out, she told Mike. When it was dismissal time Mike was standing at the front of the school with a team of older boys waiting to find the boys who'd hurt me and retaliate. Though they never found them, it was the first time I felt like my brother cared about me. He came to fight for me. That was how I defined love back then.

Several weeks later I was raped at gunpoint.

Jehovah didn't show up for me.

CHAPTER THREE

LOSING MY RELIGION

The first time I decided that Dash would be your name I was in my mid-thirties and was at a funeral for a nineteen-year-old boy who was shot to death—the same age I went to prison.

Let me tell you about my Dash.

Our Dash, because we are not well, and there is no cage or religion or God in the heavens, on Earth, or in your mind who can protect you from broken human beings.

Transferring to Martin Luther King Jr. High School was the best decision I made...or that was made for me. After my freshman year at Westinghouse, I got a safety transfer to MLK. Because of the beatdown and attempted robbery, my mom and Westinghouse figured it would be best if I went to another school. The only people at my new school who knew about the safety transfer was me. The only people in my neighborhood who knew about the safety transfer, outside of family, was me. I told my new friends at MLK, like Terrell, who would become one of my closest friends in life, that I transferred over to MLK because Westinghouse had too many boys and not enough chicks. The boys-to-girls ratio at Westinghouse was real, though. I'd be in class with thirty kids, about five or six of whom were girls. That was a believable lie to hide the feeling that I was too pussy to survive Westinghouse, which was why I had to transfer out.

During that new school year and new transfer, though, my outlook on life changed drastically. I was still fourteen years old, going to the Kingdom Hall with Daddy, still watching *Darkwing Duck* and *Saved by the Bell* on television.

On some Fridays after school I would meet Kelly at her job in Manhattan, near Thirty-Fourth Street, to tax her for some little brother money. I picked up Devon after school and took care of him until she or my mother came home from work. Kelly gave me about $20 per week and I'd save that money to buy my Timberlands and sneakers.

When I met Kelly at her job she'd usually use me as an excuse to take a break from work. This Friday was regular in that context, but this Friday's pickup was unlike any other.

We walked a few blocks to Eighth Avenue, window shopping until her break was over. We parted ways a few blocks from Times Square, the old Times Square, when peep shows were everywhere.

On my way to the train station at Forty-Second Street a brother walked out of a commercial building, locked eyes with me, and approached. He looked innocent enough. He said he was doing some moving for an office in the building and asked if I could help him out. He said he would give me a few dollars, and in an undertone asked if I smoked weed.

"Yeah, I smoke." At this point I had smoked weed a handful of times, but if a dude from the street was asking if I smoked, I knew I had to puff my chest up and say I did. He could have been a cop for all I knew, but I was too caught up in my own need to not feel like a punk. I thought I was smart enough to detect that he was not a cop. He wasn't going to think I was pussy off the rip. And he really wasn't a cop.

"Yeah, I can help you."

"Okay, wait right here. I'll be right back. Let me go back inside and then we'll walk a few blocks to get some of the other boxes at another location."

He walked back into the building, had a short conversation with someone, came back out, and told me to follow him.

We walked about two or three blocks closer to Forty-Second Street, made a right, and walked into a building. A hotel.

He told me to walk ahead of him. To a stairwell. Up several flights of steps—maybe four.

I get light-headedness, shortness of breath, dry mouth, and bubbly belly when I get extremely nervous or anxious. I was learning to conceal the jittery part good by this time.

I stopped at the top of the steps and asked, "Sir, where we going!" The exclamation in my voice was weak.

"What the fuck you asking me? Keep walking, lil nigga!" The exclamation in his voice was strong.

I lost control of the jitters.

We walked up to another flight and exited out of the stairwell into a narrow corridor. He made a fist around my arm, opened the room directly in front of the stairway, and directed me into it with the same closed grip. He walked me into the part of the room where the bed was.

The bathroom was immediately to the right once I entered. The room ahead looked unused. The beds were made, the carpet was clean, the night table was at the right side of the bed. The TV was off. I remember some light coming from the windows, or at least I think I did.

He stood in front of me, pulled out a black gun. He told me to pull down my pants. He was speaking in sentences with lots of exclamation points. I pulled my pants down. He told me to pull my underwear down.

I was really jittery. I was really light-headed. I was really dry-mouthed. And I was really bubbly belly. I could barely breathe.

I pulled down my underwear.

He placed the gun on the night table behind him.

He got on his knees, placed his hand on my joint, and began rubbing it against his face. He placed it in his mouth. He made it stand up. He took his shit out and began rubbing it back and forth. He made me feel like I was going to pee. I was uncontrollably jittery. I peed in his face.

That's what I thought I did.

I apologized for it. I thought he was gonna shoot me because of it.

After my last "sorry" I asked him if I could go to the bathroom. I pulled my underwear and pants up and walked into the bathroom, groped for the light, and closed the door.

There was no lock on the bathroom door.

I peed, wiped my tears, looked into the mirror, and asked Jehovah why he didn't help me.

I also remembered that I had a combination lock in my jeans pocket. I used to carry it just in case somebody tried to rob me, or tried to bother me. I started carrying the lock after what went down at Westinghouse.

I walked out of the bathroom, but only far enough where I could see him before he could see me, threw the lock in the direction of his face, turned around, and ran out of the room. I ran down the same steps I came up, out to the lobby, out into the street, straight to the A line at Forty-Second Street—Times Square.

Waiting for the train, I was confused. I was mad at myself for not listening to my bubbly stomach and jitters. I had started feeling them the moment he said we had to walk a few blocks. I remember walking and wanting to disappear from the situation but feeling like I needed to prove something. Like I needed to validate that I was man enough not to be scared. I think I stopped being a kid that day. My worries became more than the regular teenage things like failing classes or getting a girlfriend. I had to keep secrets that were adult.

There were so many thoughts running doggedly.

"If I tell anybody about this they gonna think I'm gay."

"I shouldn't have wanted that weed."

"Fuck Jehovah! You ain't looking out for me. Why you keep letting all these bad things happen to me?"

"Why everybody think I'm soft?"

"Why do bad things keep happening to me?"

I posed those questions to myself, no one else. I didn't know about therapy other than it was something rich white people did when they were going through a divorce, and that usually happened on TV or in the movies. Talking to someone or calling the police never occurred to me. I just held it all in and busied myself to forget about it. Acted like it never happened, although I saw the man in my nightmares and my daydreams. My body would jolt when the images of the moment crept into my daily thoughts.

I thought I was being strong by not making a big deal of it. How would I explain to anyone that I let some dude force himself onto me? Gun or no gun I convinced myself that I should have known better. Boys from the hood don't get raped, especially not fourteen-year-old boys who were almost six feet tall. I was more ashamed than anything else. By puberty I was committed to notions of manhood that were determined by how much pain I could keep to myself.

I was good at moving on and acting okay. The robberies were good training. I didn't take a day off from school to recover, or sleep it off. When I got home I showered, threw away the boxers I'd worn that day, got dressed, picked up Dev from school, came home, and played Nerf basketball with him in his room. I went to school the next day.

I moved on. Told no one. *Acted* regular.

But I knew I needed to be different. I couldn't be a victim no more. Being this good kid who went to the Kingdom Hall and sat in the front of class wasn't working for me. It didn't feel safe. I felt more insecure than ever in my performance of masculinity. I had my first high school fight a couple of weeks later because this boy named Phil from Harlem was cracking jokes about my lips. I started cutting classes with regularity to sneak into the gym to play basketball.

I avoided Daddy yelling at me for not going to the Kingdom Hall with him by being out of the house for as long as possible. I'd spend most of my evenings after school by Kofi's house. I scheduled my life to see as little of my father as possible. The life he wanted for me, to be a baptized Jehovah's Witness, was no longer attractive to me. That life wasn't protecting me, and Daddy couldn't save me from the streets because neither he nor Mommy knew my secrets.

I punished Daddy for most of my teenage years by distancing myself from him emotionally. I don't know if I saw him as a physical representation of God, but I didn't want to talk to him like the daddy's boy I used to be. The extent of our conversations were salutations like "good morning," "good afternoon," and "good night." If I needed money I would ask Mommy. One night, I came home after smoking a couple of blunts outside. My eyes were red, slanted, and glassy, and I went to the kitchen to handle my munchies when Mommy said to me with sweat in her eyes: "Marlon, what are you doing to yourself? Why are you blocking your father out? You know you hurting him. You don't even talk to him no more, and look at you, yuh eyes red fuh so. Yuh doing drugs." Then, her maxim, "Who don't hear does feel."

I felt sad for the rest of the night, then went back to my hanging out the next day, smoking the same number of blunts with my homies. My ability to disconnect from feelings became much easier. That's what sanity looked like for me. No way could I sensibly move through my day feeling the depth of the emotions that tried to surface.

Kofi, me, and our brothers on the block catcalled and tried to run trains on girls—batteries when we switched to Trini lingo. We got stopped and frisked by police. We played dominoes and spades, watched basketball and football games. We survived in spectrums of good, bad, ugly, worse, and worser.

During the summer, playing steelpan was my saving grace. It was the only hangout I had where I felt safe and creative.

Back on the block, I was no more prone to doing random, dangerous, and dumb things than most teenagers in college or in white hick towns do, but that are criminalized in Crown Heights and Flatbush. Me and my boys packed cars on Friday nights, high and drunk, looking for house parties to crash. We had guns. Some of us sold drugs. Not me, really. I sold weed for half a summer and could not control feeling dry-mouthed and light-headed. Stop-and-frisk was an everyday thing. We didn't have the nice name "stop-and-frisk" back then. Police picked on us like the dudes who robbed me, except instead of money or jewelry they stole our dignity.

Though Dev was nine years younger than me, and I was still a teen, he was the way I recaptured childhood. He was a welcome part of my daily life. Without knowing it, he gave me relevance. He was a much more vibrant and freewheeling kid than I was. He was confident, and I admired that. I felt like I needed him more than he needed me.

On some nights of steelpan practice at the panyard I'd take Dev along with me. He was my sidekick. He was the best thing I had going in my life. One evening the police stopped me and him when we got off a public bus on our block. Dev was about eight at the time, but that didn't stop four detectives in an unmarked van from stopping us.

I noticed them driving slowly behind us, so I grabbed Dev's hand to signal that I was walking with a child and not a threat. Though I was a child, too, just sixteen, I was a grown-ass man to police. Nothing could stop them from grilling us about having guns or drugs on us even though we both had on shorts and T-shirts. They told us to go home and that they were gonna watch us walk in our building. Obediently, we walked into our apartment building. When we got in the apartment we watched TV like regular, because that's what it was, a ghetto routine. I don't even think we told our parents about the stop. It was a part of our existence. I mean, we knew it was annoying, but at least they didn't frisk us. I was vexed that they stopped me while I was walking with Dev, and that we had to prove we lived where I said we did, but at least they didn't try to Abner Louima me. Louima was a Haitian immigrant who was sodomized with a plunger handle by Justin Volpe, a New York City police officer. I was aware of the possibilities with any interaction with the NYPD, and so did Dev, even at eight.

I had to be worried about both soulless police and hurting young boys my age. That same summer I was robbed at gunpoint for a small chain I paid about $69 for. Actually, I still question if the guy really had a gun in my back. When he came up to me from behind and pressed an object into my back and snapped the chain off my neck, I wasn't as scared as I thought I'd be, since it was the second time someone pointed a gun at me. After he told me not to turn around and he ran off, I just walked into my building, went by Kofi's place instead of my own, and watched TV with his younger brothers.

I felt like a punk again for letting this happen, and I was too embarrassed to tell anyone. I felt like I was too old, *at sixteen*, to let someone rob me in front of my own building. Police and peers were punking me where I lived. So what, they both carried guns? Why did they pick me?

I fought a kid on my block even when he pulled out a razor to cut me. I think a referee would say he beat me up because he got more hits in, but I know my orange and blue stripe Gap T-shirt was drenched with his blood. Maybe it was a draw.

It was around that time that I began feeling like nothing or no one could protect me or understand how I was feeling.

Losing my religion came at a high cost. I didn't know how to exist in a world outside the confines of the Kingdom Hall. The Kingdom Hall, at least at that time, implicitly discouraged young people from seeking riches in the world, which meant getting a college education only if you thought it was absolutely necessary to get a job to take care of yourself and your family. It wasn't an anti-capitalist stance, but they had an anti-government view. They paid their taxes and that was it. No voting, no military, no pledge of allegiance, just pay taxes and follow the Bible as they understood it—as I understood it too, even after I stopped wearing the label of Jehovah's Witness.

I danced with a reggae dancehall crew called Suspense, which was made up of mostly high school friends. Me, Sha, Jay, Tori, Bingi, Kev, Lil Kev', Rell, Delano, and Kofi, were Suspense. Dancing in local talent shows, block parties, and basement parties throughout Brooklyn was some of the most innocent fun I had next to steelpan. Our favorite dance was the Brukup. Rhythmically snapping the joints in our shoulders, elbow, necks, hips, and knees, and ankles to dancehall reggae was a performance for onlookers. It was joy. It was the type of fun that took me away from the stress of moving on from all the robberies, academic failures, and neighborhood violence. We dyed our hair shades of blond and auburn, and wore wide-leg jeans; and we sweated and sometimes smelled without care of judgement. We were being free Black boys.

We also hopped subway turnstiles to go to and from those parties, and the police chased us for it. We were being teens. To the police we were being criminals—fare evaders. I spent a day in jail for it.

Throughout high school I was always a great studier, test taker, and sometimes a really good cheater. I never cheated on important exams, only on the weekly or monthly ones that didn't really matter, and I could decipher when a test or a subject was frivolous to a teacher. And I loved English and history classes. I failed more classes than I passed, but I got the grades for the classes I needed in order to graduate. I was wading in the wind.

I had no idea what I wanted to do after high school. I didn't apply to any colleges, despite the advice of teachers who saw potential in me. I was too cluttered with trauma to hear them. School couldn't capture my attention anymore. The honor roll and valedictorian days from junior high were a foggy memory. I rarely did schoolwork or homework, but would read the assigned history textbooks like they were novels. History appealed to me, not because of a class requirement, but because I loved learning about the past. Still, I had no idea of the kind of job that liking history would get me. All I wanted to do was graduate on time, and I did. Even my sister's boyfriend who lived in Maryland was encouraging me to apply to a school down there. None of that was audible to me. I had no purpose, and while that's normal to most teens, a purposeless existence in the midst of serious traumas and real concerns about personal safety can be a poisonous concoction.

The summer after graduation I found out I could sit for something like a pass-fail entrance test to New York City College of Technology. I passed the test, like I knew I would, but was placed in remedial classes. I scored well enough to get into school, but not good enough to be college level. I was failing to meet my goal of mediocrity.

City Tech was my choice because my brother had taken a couple of classes there and it was close to home. It was in downtown Brooklyn, just a few stops away on the subway, so in between classes I'd come back to the block. My major was drafting. Ask me what drafting was about and I would convince you I knew what the concentration consisted of with a believable lie. I had no real college goals. College was something—a good thing—to do.

I was a boy without direction. My parents were too old to keep up with me. My sister would check in with me from time to time, but she was in her late twenties and had her own issues. Mike and I were cordial at best. We all lived in the same apartment and kept our personal pain to ourselves. We laughed and joked like all families do when avoidance of trauma is easier than crying and talking about it. Our parents provided a decent life for us and we were no longer on the dangerous Nostrand Avenue. Bringing up any personal pain would be showing ungratefulness to that progress.

None of us were sick, on drugs, or in jail. We all had our own bedrooms. Niggas weren't getting shot outside our widows anymore. Girls weren't being thrown off our roof. People weren't smoking crack in the building hallways. We were good. We were okay. Rising out of poor to poverty was our measure of success.

Hanging out on the block talking shit, smoking, drinking, and catcalling girls was my escape. The exclamation points in my sentences got even stronger.

I was about seventeen or eighteen years old when I almost ran train on a girl. I was a late bloomer. This is what boys did at hooky parties. I had never been to a hooky party, but guys always told me that chicks would be having sex with whoever was there. At least two of my boys said they lost their virginity at a hooky party, though they never named the girls they lost it to. Back then names didn't matter.

I have an indistinct image of her—Black girl, light-skinned, I think. That was all she was to me. A blank in Black girl skin. I can't say her name because she was invisible to me at the time. My father taught me better. My mommy showed me better. I ignored them like most teenage boys. The older guys probably had mothers and fathers who taught them better and showed them better, too.

But we ignored it all. We were born to know better and do better. Women, not just those who were mothers, were powerful and to be respected. Learning how to dismiss and abuse women is something we picked up along the way.

I met her in Albee Square Mall in downtown Brooklyn. My boys and I had just smoked a blunt; it was the beginning of the school year. I was rocking the new blue and gray Penny's, with a blue Karl Kani fleece. Waves were on point, too. I had the late 1990s teenage swag that day. When I smoked back then my confidence was on ten, especially when I was with my dudes. We were out to holler at bitches, that's what we called it—now I'd call it street harassment. Same thing guys do today.

We stood on the sidewalk in front of one of the jewelry stores where there was always a sale, the kind of place where we'd put a chain on layaway even though we never had the money to take it out.

Groups of girls hanging out after school were walking around *just for us to look at.* That's what we thought back then—that girls existed for our entertainment. Some of the girls thought the same thing too, we assumed, but we knew that most of them didn't want to be harassed. We chose to ignore that obvious fact because we were insecure, had no real game, and were performing for our boys—masculinity told us that we had to perform manhood at all times. It told us not to see those girls as people. To us they were titties, asses, and camel toes that also happened to walk and talk.

One group of girls *slowed down just enough for us* to receive their attention. That's what we believed back then. Girls were alive for our enjoyment. One of the girls looked in my direction, and after she walked by, I hollered, "Ayo, wassup miss." I was hoping she'd ignore me. I had no follow-up. Hollering at girls was a game most of us were afraid to win. Most of us didn't know how to keep a conversation going (though there were always one or two sexually mature guys who had Ray-J lyrics ready). We hoped that "Can I get your phone number?" as a follow-up line did the charm.

This time it worked...sort of. She took my phone number. Well, not the girl I thought walked by slowly enough *just for us to receive her attention*. It was one of the other girls in the group— one I didn't think was cute. But a girl gave me a number, and I had to impress my team so it was a win-win. Plus, she had friends, so the team assumed they were going to get hooked up too, as long as I kept in touch with the girl I didn't think was cute. No one cared to remember any of their names.

A couple of weeks later, I was with a group of friends and we were all hanging on one of the blocks in Brooklyn that we thought of as our outdoor living room.

We were bored.

One of our older friends had an apartment that all the fellas got to hang at. The apartment was another living room for all of us. It was late, not many girls were still walking by for us to harass. At some point one of the guys brought up the girl I met in the mall. They didn't know her name, and neither did I—not initially. I just knew she lived in the Marlboro Houses projects near John Dewey High School, near Coney Island, I think, where Wyclef from the Fugees was from. We had spoken once on the phone for about five minutes. I only spoke to her because in those days we didn't have caller ID. I couldn't know who was calling me, so I picked up the phone. It didn't matter what we talked about because she didn't matter to me.

We decided to call her to see if she would come over with her friends to our outdoor living room. We would then try to convince them to come into the indoor living room if they actually showed up.

She agreed and said she would bring a few of her friends.

During the forty-five minutes or so it would take for them to get to us, we had to figure out who was going to try to have sex with them. The process was no different than deciding who's going to be on your pickup basketball team. Best players get picked first. No one is concerned with who is going to play guard, forward, or center. In this case, it was about who was better at performing their masculinity; the dudes with the biggest personalities got first dibs.

When the girls arrived—three of them—it was decided that me and two of my homeboys were going to run the train with the girl who came to see me. The other fellas were going to figure out how to have sex with the other girls.

I still didn't think she was cute, but that didn't matter, the performance had already started. We were a team of "boys being boys," with all the camaraderie that goes with it. Running trains had very little to do with the girls. It was about sexual prowess. It was about bragging rights. It was about being able to have a story to tell your other boys.

We knew that if she came over to our block *at night*, then we were going to have sex with her. Maybe not necessarily with all of us, probably just me. Either way, she was invisible to us as a full human being. What mattered was that I was going to add a train story to my résumé like the other guys, something to share with the fellas.

The plan was for me to start kissing up on her and then lead her to one of the bedrooms in the apartment. Waiting in the room were the two guys who were my teammates in this battery—in the dark. Once I started having sex with her, I would move over so my boys—one at a time—would have sex with her, too.

This was how I heard it was done. I knew better and was shown better, but performing this kind of toxic masculinity—living out rape culture—was more important to all of us, and to me. Girls and women were just bodies we were taught to harass. Older guys showed us how to do it. Older guys never stopped us from doing it. It was what guys did, we thought. Hollering at chicks because we were insecure. We became practiced in *not seeing* women. We were falling in line with the bullshit that goes back to the framers of the Constitution, who chose not to see women (among other folks) as citizens and people at the birth of this nation. Book smart people call it patriarchy. All the same thing.

My girls arrived. Three of them.

We knew, without a doubt, that the girls wanted to get they freak on. I can imagine now that she could've just wanted to hang with me and brought her two friends for company or protection. We had only spoken twice on the phone, so wanting people she could trust come along with her would make sense. That possibility didn't occur to me back then.

After a bit of small talk, and according to plan, I started kissing *my* girl and got her to go into the dark bedroom. The room was cluttered with clothes, bags, and random things like broken fans and old luggage. Guys could barely find their way around the bedroom without bumping into something. So we assumed she wouldn't notice two guys hiding under clothes.

I was kissing her neck on one of the two jumbled beds. The girl was kissing me back, or I told myself she had to be. She wouldn't come here if she didn't want me to have sex with her. Back then I thought that if a girl let me kiss her that meant she also wanted to have sex, and it wouldn't be no fun if the homies couldn't get some.

My hands made their way into her jeans.

Somebody coughed. One of the other guys in the room. She heard it.

She asked, "What was that noise? Somebody else in the room?"

"I—I don't know," I responded.

One of the guys got mad at the other one for coughing and stood up.

"Why you couldn't hold that cough! I'm outta here, yo."

Before he could leave, she had pushed me to the side and rushed out of the room.

She told her friends it was time to go. They'd been sitting there with the other guys, talking. Or maybe they'd felt trapped in a house with a bunch of guys they hardly knew, a thought that didn't occur to me for years, until thinking about it now...as I remember and write.

That was it. *My* girls left our block, and I guess went back home. It really didn't matter where they went. They, their feelings, and what happened to them were invisible to us. We were more upset with the guy who couldn't hold his cough. He couldn't hold his manhood; he messed up our train—same thing.

Looking back, he probably saved us from running that train. I can't exactly say that he saved that girl, because I don't know what effect that incident had on her; whether, or how, she remembers it now. But that's definitely not something I thought about at the time.

This type of shameful behavior is as common as rocking fresh sneakers and a crisp haircut. Running trains, street harassment, and otherwise abusing girls and women has everything to do with a collective mindset that values performing masculinity for the approval of other men, with girls and women as collateral damage. Our yearning to perform for other boys and men takes place on college campuses, apartments, street corners, and malls everywhere. Most men need to admit to that.

Every day we do not admit to these things, we (re)-traumatize countless women. We are telling younger guys that it is okay. Running trains, batteries, or whatever you call it in your language or culture, is wrong. It's not masculine. It's not about manhood. It is not true camaraderie. It is deranged. It is toxic. It is predatory.

It is common.

Most men need to say that.

We need to stop blaming the woman who "should have known better" than to go to his apartment or hotel room or dorm; blaming the girls who are "hot" and "fast"; blaming the media for stirring up trouble because of a hidden agenda; blaming everyone but the men who act out the predatory masculinity enabled by the patriarchy. Justice means that we, men, listen to girls and women when they express how our seemingly harmless actions and gestures of attraction scare them. I have no idea what it's like to live in the body of a woman, and I struggle with listening to that unknowingness. My failure at hearing more often than it is fair to any of my other imperfections. But I also know that when I did what I did back then, I was acting out the worst options of my possibilities. Because of that I also know that I have so much room to be better than that, to be okay with being wrong about what I thought was normal behavior to women. Justice mandates that men be okay with being told that our actions hurt, even when we don't touch. Justice demands the restoration of dignity and a recognition of the harm done. Justice requires men to admit to the prevalence of rape and to commit to understanding and ending the harm of street harassment. Our best possibilities as men have so much room for growth. Justice is what love looks like in public, and treating women as things of invisibility is not loving.

Most men need to say that. All boys need to be taught this.

I admit that as much as I needed to be seen as fully human, I was denying the women in my life that same humanity.

CHAPTER FOUR

DASH

Dear Dash,

Everyone has a dash, even you. You are the only person who could make me jump out of sleep; the only person who could cause my body to jolt at random times when you leaped from my subconscious to my conscious. I wonder if you ever think of me. Do you ever get the same jolt as me? Do you ever wonder what happened to me after we met? Do you wonder if I ever told anyone about you? Do you ever wonder if, and how, you impacted my life? I wonder if you ever thought about how your past experiences perverted how you saw me when we met. What was your childhood like?

Why did you take my childhood away from me? Did someone take yours? You're a part of my dash—you're an indelible part of my life that has shaped the way I walk in the world. Ironically, the first time I decided to give you the name Dash was at the funeral of a young man I knew who was murdered at nineteen, the same age I was when I went to prison. The eulogist spoke about the dash on a tombstone—the day of birth to the day of your death. The speaker used the reference of the dash to ask the audience of young mourners to consider what they will have accomplished during that dash. What will they be remembered for?

I understood the analogy differently. The young man who died was a participant in an Alternatives to Incarceration program that I worked for at the time. He was a Crip, and so were most of the young people in the funeral home that day. The room was filled with teenage boys in jeans, sneakers, button-down church shirts, and dark shades to hide the sweat coming from their eyes. The girls were in their church dresses, and others were in their best house party outfits. All of them were crying, sobbing, punching their fists into their hands, gasping, whisperingly cussing to themselves, hurting. I wondered to myself about our young folks who are out here dying and fighting and surviving in gangs and on street corners. What happened to them in their lives that could have led them to become walking hurt people who hurt other people? What led me? What was that, Dash? I didn't wonder what legacy we would leave behind; I wondered, what was their trauma? Who was responsible for it? What happened to us who were all innocent once, all cute and cuddly babies? The Dash, I felt then, is the cumulative trauma that shapes us from infancy.

Who or what was a part of your Dash?

I think I saw you three or four years later as I was walking down Fulton Street in downtown Brooklyn. You were standing on the street, seemingly unbusy. I think you saw me, too. I was bigger by then. I had held and shot guns off roofs. I knew people who I could get to beat the shit out of you. I could beat you by myself. But....

But I was too ashamed to approach you. What if you said it never happened? What if you tried to embarrass me by saying out loud that I was a "faggot-ass nigga"? What if I hit you and was arrested? How could I explain why I had hit you?

How could I explain that the first time I ever busted a nut it was with you at gunpoint? That would earn me no hood stripes. Fourteen-year-old men should be able to defend themselves. It was my fault. I wanted a bag of weed. I shouldn't have been smoking weed. I was a Jehovah's Witness. I was trying to be helpful by helping you move the boxes. How could a kid from 1990s Brooklyn where gunshots flew by every day be so gullible? Why did you exploit my ignorance? Who or what exploited yours?

Did you ever wonder what type of student I was in school? Did you know I was close to honor roll that year? That I had been a valedictorian three years before we met? How were you in school?

Did you know that just a couple months before we met I was jumped so badly in school that I couldn't go back for a couple weeks? They tried to rob me. When I told one of the three boys that I had nothing to give them, and pushed his hands away from my front jeans pockets, they beat me dizzy. I had to get a safety transfer from George Westinghouse High School. I told my new friends at Martin Luther King Jr. High School that I transferred there because King had more girls than boys, and I wanted to be where the chicks were at. I lied. I was ashamed. It was manhood shit, or the toxic masculinity thing that smart feminists talk about; words and terms I never heard about until

I was in my thirties, concepts that surviving street shit and prison shit did not allow for. It meant that I would use wanting to be around girls as an excuse for the deep hurt—physically, but more so emotionally—that being jumped brought on. Then, too, I thought I should have been able to better defend myself, or my walk should have been tougher, or my clothes should have been more baggy like '90s rappers, or I should smoke weed because that's what tough niggas did, or maybe I should carry a gun, or a knife, or a razor, or maybe I should cuss more, or maybe some other fake masculine shit I learned from walking on Nostrand Avenue in 1990s Crown Heights, that eventually landed my ass in prison facing a life sentence.

I kept this truth a secret until I put these words in this passage. At thirty-eight years old, that fake masculine shit no longer works for me. It ain't real. It took me way too long to outgrow the idea that manhood shit, that toxic masculinity, that being harmed has nothing to do with my personal weakness but more about your personal weakness.

What was your personal weakness?

Did you know that I would have rather kept you a secret? Did you keep me a secret? Did you ever feel like you had to keep someone or something tragic a secret?

Years after we met in Midtown Manhattan I was shot and kept the details of the shooting secret. Jerked off for the first time at eighteen years old because I thought it was a sin, so I kept it a secret from Jehovah and my father. Got robbed at gunpoint for a chain on my own block when I was sixteen years old, and kept that a secret for—well, until now, because I thought I was a pussy for letting that happen. Felt I'd die before twenty-one, and kept the reasons why I felt that way a secret.

At eighteen years old I almost pulled off a train—a rape—on a chick without her knowledge. Almost went to prison for life, and kept the details of my involvement in the crime a secret for years. I became the harmer. The persons hurt by me were not weak. I was. I was dealing with the shit that you were— are—dealing with.

Did you know that I was fourteen years old, and fourteen-year-old boys who think they are fourteen-year-old men should not have to keep such heavy and traumatic secrets? Did you have to keep heavy secrets as a kid? Did you think you were a fourteen-year-old man, too?

Are you still alive? Have you found the help you needed? Or did you continue to act out your pain—whatever it was? Did you wonder what became of me? Did you know I still think about you; that I am still ashamed; that I still blame myself some-times; that I still jolt; that you can still wake me from my sleep? I somehow never hated you, though I hated the memory of you.

Did you know that I have successfully compartmentalized you and have thrived despite not yet coming to grips with my emotional deadness to intimacy? Were you able to perform being aight as well as I do? I hurt those closest to me with emotional distance, but I perform being aight to the world masterfully.

In peace,

Marlon,

You hurt me

I'm like America. America, he hurts people all over the world every day. Weakness seeks out the strength in others to support its own fragility. I was being American. America the beautiful founded on masculinity and grit. America the indivisible that saw hope and fortune for itself in manifest destiny. America is me —a lie that supports its original injustice. Being dishonest with self.

What was your Dash?

What occurred in your life that would allow you to act out the worst parts of your humanity?

Since we last saw each other my facade of aightness has made me something of a role model. Like most of us hurt people who find a way to step away from but not out of our hurt, I have been exceptionalized as one of those *Black men who have risen like a Phoenix; though, most people don't realize that a Phoenix rises from the soot of its predecessor. The effects of the soot that choked New York City for months after the 9/11 attacks remain. Some experts have said that the medical risks from the soot from 9/11 will not develop for some people until about twenty-five to thirty years after the initial exposure. Word, even if the soot is no longer visible, its stench and residue remain.*

What was your 9/11? Your stench changed me.

CHAPTER FIVE

OKAY

"Dear Daddy," it began... "Daddy, promise to never share this letter or tell anyone about this letter. I don't even want you to ever bring it up in conversation with me. Don't ever ask me any questions about the incident... ever. I just needed to tell someone that this happened and that I am okay. If you ever mention this to anyone I will never trust or forgive you."

—Love you forever, Your son

Okay is an overused word. It can wear any personality. Okay can mean anything and it can mean nothing. It can connote that life is good, life is a terrible struggle, or life is too confusing to put into words, or I have a secret that I wish I knew how to express but can't.

It's like we are trapped in a word of nothingness. Lies, that's what they are. This is a country of broken systems imagined by the hollowness of white men. Some of y'all call it white supremacy, but whatever. There was never a time in America when the massive number of Black people weren't in chains of some kind. The death penalty by lynching was the predecessor to incarceration.

No one is okay under these conditions. But we contort ourselves into believing that America helps more than it harms.

I didn't know or understand any of this in 1998. I was just happy I finally lost my virginity. There was no concern for the girl I was with or the act itself. My waves was fly and I hadn't had any school or neighborhood problems in almost two years. I had just turned eighteen.

The first time I held a gun I was fourteen or fifteen years old. My homeboy's uncle, just three years older, pointed one at me late one night for jokes. I was the butt of the joke. The three of us were smoking weed in his room, when the uncle pulled out the gun, pointed it toward me, and said, "Get the fuck out of here. Nigga! I said get the fuck out of here or ima shoot you, nigga!"

I was dry-mouthed, but I suppressed the jittery light-headedness. I was much better at masking by then. But I still got up and hauled ass up out of that narrow and poorly lit room.

After a few seconds they started laughing. "You pussy, Sun. How you believe I was gon' shoot you? For what? Hahaaaaaa."

I laughed, too. I was aight, I thought. "They were just playing with me."

"Or were they 'playing' me?"

I wasn't okay.

That first semester of college I got a hookup with a telemarketing job from my older cousin, Camika. She had come up from Trinidad on a student visa a few years earlier and stayed with us on St. Marks Avenue for a few months. She had become a supervisor at a telemarketing call center and she "nepotized" a brother. That job would find its way back to me years later.

I saved up enough to go to Trinidad Carnival off my own money, not my parents'. I started washing my own clothes at fourteen because I remember thinking that I was too old for my mother to wash my clothes. I yearned for independence.

Kofi and I had plans to wine up on every girl in Port of Spain. I definitely think I came close. He probably did, too. I didn't have ten cents worth to save my life, but I knew how to converse with a wine. I could move my waist in the way Trinidadian men do to make it look fluid and musical. I loved to dance and listen to soca music. I was Trinidadian at heart.

I spent most of the trip with Kofi's family. His parents were Trini like mine, and Kels was close to his family, too. We all became play cousins the way Black people all over the world create extended families every place we go.

Back in Brooklyn, because we liked the same music, Kofi and I cooked up the idea to start deejaying. As a child, I'd have the radio on 1190 AM WLIB, where Saturdays and Sundays were strictly Caribbean music. I grew up listening to Chalkdust, Sparrow, Kitchener, Denyse Plummer, and a kid artist named Machel Montano. Kofi, too. His uncle had some old deejay equipment, and we put money together to buy a mixer and records. We called our set Mystik Sounds. Reggae, dancehall, hip-hop, soca, and R&B was the music we liked, so that's what we played.

We practiced in his bedroom with headphones, like Q in *Juice*. We got good enough to play at a few house parties. I was Skeez and he was Jaga Dan.

My boy Rell gave me the name Skeez back in high school. He had a penchant for giving people names and titles that fit the perception he had of the person. In tenth grade there were two girls who liked me and I think I liked them too, so Rell started calling me Skeezer, which quickly became Skeez. I defined Skeez as a little sneaky, reckless, more visible. Skeez walked with knives and sometimes hammers, like a real-ass hammer. I'm so happy I never had a chance to test whether I would actually use either. I think Skeez could have, though. He boosted sneakers and clothes, and did some other stupid teenager things that don't need to be mentioned here.

Skeez was a version of myself that no one saw coming. But he was here, and he made me feel freer. Liberated from the insecurity of having big lips and feelings that I was soft. He was the best mask I ever had because he made it so easy to disguise Marlon. There were always three of us. No, not in the schizophrenic, multiple personalities' way. *I* would reason with Skeez and ignore Marlon. I had a ghetto-ass Holy Trinity. *I* is the person who always knew that a choice was available. *I* is also the person whose voice wasn't trained up to speak with exclamation points, so *I* was never heard. Skeez did a lot of dumb adult shit in Marlon's teenage body. A higher level of stupidity started happening after we came back home from the Trinidad Carnival trip.

The second semester of college was back in session. I decided to take school seriously this time around. I went to classes more often than I had the semester before, and I spent less time on the block doing random teenage things. I was eighteen, a freshman, had a part-time telemarketing job, and was more concerned about feeling like a sucker and a pussy whenever I saw homies around the way who knew I was punched and robbed for my chain. I wore that memory like glasses. The trauma shaped how I saw the world. No amount of distractions, college included, could take me away from what was most important to me then: safety and reputation. Although it had been over six months since the robbery, every day felt like the day after it happened. Losing at manhood stung hard and festered, even though I was still a child. Unhealed wounds can spread like cancer. The benign ones are the most insidious because you don't realize you're an asymptomatic patient in a society with little patience for wounded Black boys.

I'm not sure how I became a symptomatic Black boy, but I learned from whom and where you could get guns. I never owned or sold a gun, but I often had possession of one, or sometimes two. I held them for friends, or directed neighborhood comrades to where they could get a good deal. Even back then I was attracted to being a connector.

The extent of my gun action was shooting them off roofs or in the park. July Fourth and New Year's were the holidays for shooting. Halloween was a good one, too.

Several weeks into the semester, on a Thursday, me and two of my boys from the block got word that we could get an almost new, out the box .25 caliber gun at a bodega we frequented. I think the price was somewhere between $100 and $150. We got the money together, bought the gun, brought it back to the block, and went on the hunt for bullets. We didn't have any specific beef, but the neighborhood was changing. Lots of dudes were becoming Blood. Nine Trey was bleeding through my neighborhood. I wasn't familiar with organized gang culture like the kind that cut across neighborhoods. Most dudes had blocks, avenues, projects, or corner bodegas that they represented. Bloods cared about Bloods. They were recruiting kids like the military did, only their potential wars were against themselves or the boy they went to elementary school with but who lived on a different block. I ain't never cared that much about any location that I felt the need to defend it like a child I made. And I did not care for Bloods. But we had no real issues other than prolonged stares of intimidation that we used to mask our fear. At sixteen, seventeen, and eighteen most of us boys were confused, scared of standing out, in need of attention, hiding pain, and burying joy.

We were hood niggas. Some of us were knee deep in the worst the streets could offer. Most others like me were curious about the possibilities the streets provided, like status among our peers. Who doesn't want to be recognized for their existence by their social group?

The options for acknowledgment were not always bountiful and visible. I was exposed to writing, history, the arts in music, steelpan, and dancing, but none of that outweighed the need to feel safe in my own neighborhood—in the world as I knew it back then.

My social group understood violence and proximity to violence as the currency for street care.

Buying that gun was street recognition.

And street recognition is like filling a bucket with holes with water. The bucket empties quickly. It is never full. No one is ever full.

After the three of us got back to the block with our new toy, we went to an apartment of one of our older homies to figure out bullets. After a call or two we got our seller. He had a whole box of .25 caliber bullets for sale. The seller, a boy who was sixteen years old, two years younger than me and lived a floor under me on the fifth floor of my building, told us to come to his crib for the transaction.

The three of us, including me as Skeez, went to my building, got into the elevator, and within five or ten seconds the gun went off. I thought it was unloaded, or maybe the idea of getting shot by my friend, by mistake, would never happen.

But, it did.

I felt an intense pressure in my right foot, but I didn't see anything in my Nike Air Max, just a small pea-sized hole in the big toe area. I fell backward onto my friend who was standing behind me in the elevator. The other friend had the gun in his hand, still facing down. Mortification was in his eyes. We had access to a neighbor's apartment on the second floor of the building, so we went there instead of the bullet supplier's apartment on the fifth floor.

And I was limping, still walking, but struggling. I didn't see any blood. Yet.

My two friends walked me to a couch in the apartment. I sat, laid my right leg to the edge of the couch arm. My friend, the one who shot me, unlaced my white and yellow Air Max's that I had stolen from an athletic store I'd worked in over the past summer.

Blood. As soon as the sneakers came off blood began drowning my white socks. I felt fire. It felt like someone was holding a torch near the knuckle of the big toe. I didn't cry, though.

Not yet.

Like kids who had done something so bad that they wanted to hide away from their parents, we decided to walk back down the block to a friend who had a car who could take me to the hospital. We were too scared to call an ambulance. One of my friends was undocumented at the time, so he was scared that if anyone found out he would get deported. None of us wanted that. So, with my sneakers back on, I started walking as fast as I could alongside my two friends.

When I finally got to the hospital—the same one my nephew, Dev, was born in—a nurse actually said I had to wait a little bit before I got seen by the doctor. Whether it was five minutes or five hours, I can't see how asking someone with a gunshot wound to wait makes for good hospital standards.

It was closer to five minutes.

During the initial intake they told me and my two friends that they would have to notify the police. Apparently, there was some rule that police had to be called to the hospital anytime someone came in with a gunshot wound. We were all frightened by that news. I didn't want my boy to get arrested and deported, and, more important, I didn't want my parents to know.

So when the police came we lied. We gave them an out of this world story about how we were playing basketball in the park when some guys started shooting in our direction, and as we were running I got shot *on the top of my foot*. Yeah, it didn't make sense and I'm pretty sure the cops knew we were lying. But they gave me their card and left. I never heard from them again. I was glad they didn't care about us.

I eventually spent a week in the hospital after having surgery to repair my foot. My friends and I decided we'd tell our families that I broke my foot playing basketball. We were scared of getting in trouble from our parents. We were kids living adult lives. My friends visited me once, or maybe twice, while I was in the hospital. It was only seven days so I guess they did their part.

As the doctor was processing me out, with my mother next to him, he said, "The way the bullet went in and popped back out... he'll walk fine again, but will likely have a limp, and won't be able to run as fast or jump as high if he plays basketball." Mommy's eye opened up real big like.

"Wha'? Marlon, you ain tell me about you get shot." It would be years before I told my family the real story of how I was shot. They knew I was lying, but I was too afraid and ashamed to tell them that I got shot because I wanted to be around guns.

I did physical therapy maybe once, and figured out my own re-hab. I smoked lots of weed, watched *Con Air* about twenty times, and masturbated a lot. I did some exercises, too, but not more than the other things. I recovered in about four months, ahead of the six-to-eight-month recovery time suggested by my doctor. In the years since then I have run half marathons, dunked and reverse dunked basketballs. I proved the doctor wrong. But to this day I still get sharp pains in the area of the gunshot at random moments when lying down.

I saw images of the sexual assault during this recovery. It was the first time I allowed myself to think about it. I wish I'd told someone that I was feeling more pain than the hole in my foot, but I didn't. I got better. I was able to play a little basketball by the end of summer.

I was aight, but not really.

Because of the rehab time I had to unenroll from school that se-mester. Once I was strong enough to move around with crutches, I started carrying that same .25 caliber in my below-the-knee cast. Whatever logic I thought I had back then was deeply warped. Po-lice wouldn't search my cast on a stop-and-frisk, I reasoned.

The year 1998 quickly became the worst of my life to that point. It got worse than 1993 when my childhood was stolen by a broken man. The ensuing summer in Brooklyn was especially hot for me. At one point I became paranoid about going outside on

Thursdays because too much was happening to me on those days that year.

I broke my right elbow one Thursday afternoon playing basketball in Brower Park across the street from my apartment building. Someone clipped my leg when I was going up for a rebound. I landed elbow-first on the concrete. I actually kept playing with the excruciating pain until the pickup game of Utah ended. My parents told me to go to the hospital immediately, but I stubbornly waited about a week before I followed their counsel. X-rays determined I was walking around with a broken elbow for almost a week. The doc gave me a sling and a prescription for the pain. Life went on.

The broken elbow was annoying because I was playing steelpan that summer, as I had done the past three years. This was the first year I played the six-bass. My first three summers I played a tenor pan, but I decided to change because the year before during practice I'd picked up an empty Heineken bottle to hit one of the band elders because I'd felt embarrassed. He had called me out in front of the entire band and ordered me to play a difficult part without the rest of the band. Maybe a note of mine was off, but my brittle self-image could not accept correction. I interpreted his revision as trying to punk me. Even though he was about thirty years older than me, I had developed a good enough mask to defend the sense of masculinity I felt I had to perform at a moment's notice.

"I ain't soft! You trying to fucking play me! I goh fuckin' buss yuh head with this bottle, you old as pussy nigga!" My exclamations were fully grown.

Thankfully, someone held me back and calmed me down. I don't think I would've hit him, but I needed to prove to everyone watching that I could. He was right. I didn't have the music down the way I should have. But I was also right. I wasn't soft in his eyes or the rest of the people in the band. I *felt* soft.

They kicked me out of the band that night, but I couldn't have felt prouder. Yeah, pan was the place that took me away from the volatility of everyday happenings in my neighborhood during the summer months, but my penetrable wall of toughness was worth the brief banishment. How I needed to be seen was way more important than how I felt. Reputation meant more to me than peace of mind. I could have no peace of mind without a reputation that protected me from being seen as prey.

I eventually apologized to him and the leaders of the band. I was wrong for my actions and I knew it. But no one there harassed me again. The price I paid was not being the best tenor pan player I could be. Who would want to mentor a kid who'd be willing to crack a Heineken bottle over your head when he disagreed with your teaching method?

I switched to the six-bass and a different band the following summer. The six-bass felt more like my speed, and I was learning to play it really well until the elbow accident. Sonatas Steel Orchestra was the name of the band. The panyard, what Trinidadians call the place where we practice, was located across the street from the school where I experienced my first robbery—IS 390. I wasn't as scared as I used to be. All the prior years, pan was nothing more than an extracurricular activity that got me away from the stress of my block. With Sonatas, pan served as a place I needed to be. I fell in love with pan that year.

In this moment of summer peace I met a girl named Shareema whose sweet kisses soothed like the salve of steelpan music—like the deep roll of my six-bass. Shareema played the double-second pan, which could play the lead, harmony, cords, or countermelody. My nephew, who was about ten at the time, played in the same band with me, and he was the one who asked Shareema to be my girlfriend. Dev was such a cool kid. Even at ten he knew how to be confident in himself. I admired him for it. He wasn't following in my footsteps, and that made me proud. I would always tell him, "My goal is to make sure you're better than me." As a teen I already believed I was deeply flawed.

One night I asked Dev to give Shareema a note; the famous, "will you be my girlfriend note" with check boxes for options:

❏ Yes
❏ No
❏ Maybe

He was supposed to do it after I left the panyard that night, but he did it damn near in front of me. She said "yes" to a boy so shook that he had to ask his baby nephew to do his bidding. Shareema was almost three years younger than me. I, eighteen, her fifteen and a half, me teetering on statutory rape levels. The way she played her double-second was so freaking attractive. She played with speed, clarity, power, and whined her waist with rhythmic precision and sensuality. Our pan love lasted a whole two months, and would rekindle over a decade later, but by that time life had happened to us both. I was in recovery mode when we met as adults, and I was out of tune and out of touch with what love and rhythm required. I lied to her and became a better Black man at her expense.

Falling in melody with Shareema as an eighteen-year-old coincided with the first time I connected peace of mind with pan. I learned the chromatic scale and could play with my eyes closed, slow-sip a Heineken, and dance with the instrument serving as my partner in melody. I felt safe there. The six-bass, four-bass, cellos, guitar pans, double tenors, tenors, double seconds—all iterations of the same steelpan but with different sounds, octaves, and tones, using what was once nothing more than an empty oil drum fit for a garbage dump—created a unison of music that gave me order. My American friends called it pots and pans clinking. Offensive as those sentiments were, none of it phased me. My peace wasn't their peace. They had their own experiences of bliss and I had mine. It was me and my pan and that's all that mattered to me. I could rock away in my Brooklyn despite the moments when Brooklyn didn't care for me. My Brooklyn made music despite it all.

About two or three Thursday nights later, I was walking home from the panyard by myself. As I approached my block I heard a ruckus from the other side of the block, which was geographically known as "up the block" by everyone who lived on St. Marks Avenue. My first instinct was not to go up the block, to go straight home. But I heard the voice of one of my younger homeboys, Shaun, who I looked at as a little brother at the time. He was Kofi's younger cousin by two years, and against our wishes, he became Blood. Gang affiliated or not, I had the sense of loyalty that I got your back even if you doing something I wouldn't do.

I didn't listen to my better judgment.

With my right arm in the sling, I walked up the block and saw that Shaun was in the middle of the street in an intense argument with some grown-ass man who didn't look familiar to the block. They were arguing because the man was a drunk driver who had driven his jeep into someone's parked car on the street. The jeep left a small dent and no one was hurt. But there was a group of boys from the block anxious to hurt him. Most of the boys were Blood and looked bored. My intuition sensed that the driver was about one sentence or volatile move from getting jumped. One of the girls told me the driver was drunk. He looked more like tipsy than piss drunk to me.

I involved myself into the argument because Shaun was sixteen and lanky. The tipsy dude looked to be about two hundred pounds. I wasn't much bigger than Shaun, but when that grown-ass man directed the wrong words in my direction, I punched him with my left hand so many times that I broke my hand. It took two days before the pain was too much to bear and I took myself to the hospital. My hand was broken so bad that I had titanium placed in it to reinforce the bone that was broken in half.

So here I was with a broken left hand and broken right elbow after finally recovering from a gunshot in my right foot. I was a crash dummy. The labor required to be seen as tough was taking a toll on my body. I was committed to my own demise in the pursuit of safety, even if it meant that parts of my physical person had to be altered by more wounds. This is what living with unaddressed wounds as a kid can look like. This is one way, not the only way. No Band-Aids to slow down the bleeding that was going everywhere on everyone.

One day after I came out of surgery, another Thursday, I was robbed and jumped around the corner from my block. I was walking with my nephew, two of his little friends, Kofi, and one of his older cousins. We were on our way to the panyard. Kofi played with Sonatas, too. I was wearing a gold chain that my mother had bought for me earlier that year when she went to Trinidad.

We were one street away from our block when several boys approached us—me. Both of them lived up the block from me. One of them, J, was one of the kids who chased me home from school when I was going to PS 138. As we got older we would walk past each other in the street with the stares of curious hostility. We knew we didn't like each other, but since it was about a decade since fifth and sixth grade, I'm not sure if we knew why we were still hostile. He was the one who punched me while another boy, who was the Blood superior at the time, yapped the gold chain my mother had bought for me. There was another boy with them on a bike, and he flinched to hit me too, but didn't. I couldn't lift my hand up to defend myself, and my two friends who I saw as family did nothing.

There is an unwritten code in the streets that you always fight if somebody brings beef to your people, especially if you are with them at the time the beef comes. This is beyond the streets, this is just friendship.

Dev, ten years old at the time, screamed at my friends, "Y'all not gonna help my uncle?" That stung. Those guys, who I knew, robbed me, put their hands on me in front of my nephew, and my friends did nothing. Nothing.

I started to run after the guys, but I quickly remembered that I was incapable of fighting. When I got back to my apartment, I made a few phone calls, and I had a gun ready for me to use. I knew where one of the guys lived.

Everything in my soul wanted to disappear from embarrassment. It was a hot summer day, everyone was outside, they all knew I got robbed, and they all knew who did it. I wanted to kill them. That was the first time in my life I felt the desire to shoot someone. The enticement was easy. I was too broken. Hiding too much pain. No one was saving me. And I didn't care about living. Most of my teenage years I was worrying about surviving. Getting through the day. Staying away from Thursdays.

The only reason I did not follow through on shooting anyone that day is that I had no strength to pull a trigger. I could barely give a handshake. My body was in pieces, too.

As the days of pain passed by, the urgency for revenge slowed but didn't disappear. I walked with the pain of knowing I had been humiliated in my neighborhood by people who lived there. It ate at me from the inside. My friends had abandoned me when I needed their protection, when I couldn't protect myself. I was living day-to-day with invisible and visible trauma.

I left the neighborhood to spend a few days by my friend Zoop without telling anyone, including my family. My plans were to let the tension die down, then shoot up the apartment of the Blood superior's mother. I knew where she lived and I wanted him to feel just as scared as I did. I wanted his mother to feel the same pain I did. I was a coward.

I was lost.

When I returned back home I told Kels that I didn't think I was going to live to see twenty-one. I felt it. I didn't know how I was going to die, but all signs lead to an early death for me. Tears welled up in my big sister's eyes as she begged me, "Marlon, why are you saying that? What's wrong? Is somebody after you? Please don't say that. Please."

I couldn't say what I believed to be true.

I felt so ashamed walking in my neighborhood every day. I imagined everyone thought I was a punk so I hung out elsewhere more often. I spent my time doing random silly teenage things on Dean Street with my older cousins or on Eastern Parkway where my high school friends lived.

It was around this time that I started hanging around Nadia and her friends. Older than me by a few years, Nadia was real close with my brother and older cousins; they considered her family. She seemed too old, maybe too mature, to have any real interactions with me. Like I said, we hung around with each other, not with each other. But for whatever reason, people seemed to listen when she spoke. At first glance, she looked like a cutie from the block that I'd catcall if I didn't know her, but knowing her made me feel like hollering at her on the street to get her number would end up with her embarrassing me somehow. So Nadia was just a girl from around the way who seemed above the shit. Years later Nadia would be a light that helped me transform my outlook on life.

I was closer to her friend Shenae. Shenae and I had a flirtatious relationship at best. We'd walk to the Nostrand Avenue train station every morning on our way to school; her to her fashion school, me to my air conditioning and refrigeration school. On one of our many train rides together, she said, "Marlon, you look and dress like an intelligent thug," and that made my day. I was being seen in a way that felt safe and tough at the same time. I wish I had listened to other things Shenae would later say to me.

At the same time, as I started spending more of my time away from St. Marks Avenue, I distanced myself from Kofi and his family. I didn't feel safe around them. I felt like I saw them as family and they saw me as another neighbor. We were not aligned.

That was the last of the unfortunate events of the summer for me. I tried to re-enroll in college in the fall but was told that I owed

$1,500 for missing the previous semester. I didn't have that money and I assumed that my parents had other things to do with their money so I didn't ask them. Looking back, I think they would have found a way to pay the outstanding balance, but I felt too prideful to ask. I also had not told them that I was on academic probation. They trusted that I would figure it out because I always managed the things that were important. I held part-time jobs, I washed my own clothes, I graduated from high school without them ever having to make me go to school or do the necessary schoolwork.

It had become easy, by then, to lie to my parents. After they found out I was shot, I pushed them away from me. I knew I was shaming them. Sometimes I cared for their feelings, sometimes I didn't. If ours was a white household, I would be seen as a bratty kid who was acting out. I was Black, so I was on my way to jail or dead. Like I told Kels, I bet on dead.

I used to daydream about what people would say about me at my funeral. Feeling unnecessary is a terrible thing. Fantasizing about my funeral had nothing to do with dying and everything to do with needing to hear my friends and family say good things to me about me. Maybe that's why rappers like Biggie and Tupac rhymed so much about death. We can't seem to get around being invisible men.

And I wanted the Blood dude who took my chain to feel pain. I wore the back-bending weight of embarrassment every day. I mean, people got robbed every day back then. That's how it got down. And I felt emasculated in a chain of events that were very sad and very hurtful and very secret. You mix a bruised sense of manhood with a fragile ego and you get all types of danger.

Two weeks before my twentieth birthday in October 1999, the first time Donald Trump considered running for president, Skeez made another dumb decision. I went on a robbery where four people were shot, two fatally.

None of it made sense. I played hooky from trade school the day of the robbery. Shenae called me that morning to say she was ready to meet for our daily walks to the Nostrand Avenue train station. I said I wasn't going to school. She asked why. I made up a lie. The truth was that I wanted to hang out with my peoples. Most days that I skipped school my excuse was to smoke weed or I was too tired from hanging out the night before. That day, a robbery was the agenda item that was more important than school.

The prosecutor in our criminal case described us as a "Trinidadian posse." Far from it. Yeah, all of us in that packed four-door sedan were Trinidadian; I was the only one not born there. But we weren't a posse, a gang, a crew, homies, or friends. We were nineteen- and twenty-year-olds who were all deadly silent in the tinted black Ford Escort on the drive from Brooklyn to Lower Manhattan. The driver got lost trying to find the Williamsburg Bridge from Crown Heights. No one offered him directions. The only sound came from Angie Martinez's voice on HOT 97.

I was the lookout. Didn't matter that my eyesight was in bad shape since I was nine. The robbery of a store in Manhattan during the day looked like an easy enough gig.

I had initially wanted to carry a gun, but that was vetoed out because they figured it wasn't necessary to carry a third gun. That's one decision I am grateful was made for me. Where I was to stand was also decided for me. They positioned me across the narrow street from the store that was to be robbed. I didn't even know what type of store it was. It was 5 p.m. on a bright fall day in Little Italy. Gentrifiers call it SoHo now. Chic-dressed people, who looked like smiling was easier than my squints and frowns, were drinking coffee in Central Perk–like cafes with bowl-sized cups. I didn't know what a latte or cappuccino was. I didn't know about *Friends* either.

When two of the guys I was with entered the store for the robbery, I walked into another store where I was positioned.

"Dred, just talk to de people in de store and keep acting busy. That's all you have to do."

My position, which was a boutique-type storefront across the narrow street, was where I attempted to act busy. I was wearing only one of my contact lenses for a prescription I'd had since the fourth grade, so I wasn't physically qualified to be a "lookout," but, in my mind, I figured, "*What was the worst thing that could happen?*"

I was supposed to act busy, but before I could get out a full sentence to the one person in the store, gunshots rang out from inside the store that my soon-to-be co-defendants were in.

From where I was, I could see people running in all directions. It was chaos, people were crying and screaming. Everyone was as jittery and frantic as I was, and I started running in the direction that seemed best. Behind me, I saw two men shooting at my soon-to-be co-defendants. I had no idea what was happening. What happened in the store? Why were people shooting at my boys from across the street? Who were *those* shooters?

I hopped on the train and went back to Brooklyn where I saw a news update on NBC 4NY. Four people were shot. Two dead. One of the deceased was a white store owner who was known for feeding unhoused people in the area. The other was a Black man who worked at the café. The two wounded people were also employees; one had been grazed by a bullet, another lost a testicle.

The worst that could have happened had happened.

Some researchers define a mass shooting as three or more shooting victims (not necessarily fatalities), not including the shooter. The shooting must not be identifiably gang, drug, or organized crime related.[1] My day off from trade school ended in a mass shooting. Shenae went to school and ended up becoming a millionaire in the fashion game.

Three days later police arrested me in front of my apartment and in front of my parents, Mike, Kels, and little Dev. I didn't think the police were after me. Even though I went along with the robbery I didn't shoot anyone, try to shoot anyone, didn't have a gun, and wasn't in the store where the robbery took place. But with a felony murder crime none of that matters. I was an active participant in one part of the robbery, which made me culpable to all parts of the incident.

In the cuffed car ride to jail, the police parked the car under the Manhattan side of the Manhattan Bridge. Plainclothes detectives took turns cursing and threatening me for a confession. I kept telling them, "I just want to go home." After about an hour of this charade they regrouped and drove me to the 5th Precinct in the Chinatown section of Manhattan. I later found out that the detectives wanted to question me before I got to the precinct because my family had already said that they were calling a lawyer. They weren't bluffing, except the lawyer was a divorce attorney who was the friend of a friend of the family.

When I finally got to the precinct I saw the two guys who'd remained in the car after the three of us had exited to do the robbery. Apparently, they had been arrested a day or two before me, meaning that I was the last person arrested of the five. The two guys who entered the store, and who eventually received forty-five and fifty years to life, were arrested at the scene of the crime. The two men who were shooting at my co-defendants were under-cover narcotics cops. They'd just happened to be in the area on an unrelated drug investigation. They'd spotted my co-defendants running away from the place of the attempted robbery, pursued them, then arrested them.

I told the police I went with my cohorts on the robbery but didn't do anything. That confession, along with an eyewitness who said I cursed her out while inside the store I was positioned at, was enough to get me indicted on a range of charges from first degree murder to criminal weapons possession. Right before arraignment my divorce attorney lawyer said that I was facing the death penalty, but that I shouldn't worry about that because the Manhattan district attorney, Robert Morgenthau, was against the death penalty, so life without parole is the worst I could get.

Thirty-one days before I was arrested I had celebrated my first Panorama[2] win, with an arrangement of "In My House" by the legendary steelpan arranger, Clive Bradley, with Pantonic Steel Orchestra. I developed my love for steelpan by watching my brother, Mike. When I was a little kid, he'd play videotapes of Panorama competitions in Trinidad when we were home alone. We didn't talk to each other much back then, but whether he knew it or not, he was communicating his love for the music of the instrument. He knew every drop in the song the steelband was playing. We didn't have a steelpan in the house, but the way he mimicked the movement of the tenor players on the TV with his homemade tenor pan sticks gave the impression that the air of his sticks was aligned with the sounds on the video.

Kels introduced me to the panyard at the same time that I was admiring Mike's love for the music. I was her tagalong little brother in the summer months when she played pan. Flatbush Avenue and Woodruff Avenue was the home of Golden Stars Steel Orchestra, where Kels played pan as a teenager. The panyard always had the aroma of corn soup, cigarettes, Heineken beer, Jheri curl moisturizer, incense, and weed. My little friends there all played tag while the older kids played their instruments. It was my version of a summer vacation.

Thirty-one days before I was arrested I was celebrating winning the same Panorama championship that Mike and Kels had won multiple times. Steelpan connected me to them. We all loved the same thing, and they taught me how to find happiness and peace playing steelpan.

My best dreams during my early years in prison were memories of playing pan. Music was one of the ways I survived prison.

The day before the robbery I was three months away from graduating from Apex Technical School as an air conditioning and refrigeration tech. I had enrolled seven months earlier because I had gotten tired of hanging around the neighborhood doing nothing after I'd dropped out of college. I remember thinking that I was getting my life together by taking the AC course. Job placement and your own set of tools were promised upon graduation. I had already started collecting the phone numbers and addresses of companies I would apply to on my own as I got closer to graduation. I'd copy the numbers from the sides of air conditioning and refrigeration company vans rolling through busy Manhattan. The robbery was just a thing to do after school before I went home to play video games with my nephew. I was a failure at performing the one foot in, one foot out thing.

Anyways, now I was facing life in prison. Not the death penalty. That was the bright side.

As for my arraignment, which took place almost two days after I was arrested, I didn't remember much, other than the judge saying that I would be *reprimanded* until my next court date. I didn't know what that meant. I thought I would be released once I saw the judge, because I didn't see why I was being held for just being with people who tried to rob a store. No money was ever taken. Apparently, my boys never got to the money.

As I was escorted out of the courtroom by an officer, I asked him what the judge meant by reprimand.

"Reprimand? You sure she didn't say *remand*?"

"Oh, yeah. I think that's what she said. What does that mean?"

"You ain't got no bail, kid. You're going to Rikers Island."

Jail was hell.

CHAPTER SIX

911

*"In life you get to choose your choices, but you
don't get to choose your consequences."*
—Marlon

Jails are designed to disorient. Your relationship to time, space,
and diet alters dramatically. Time is replaced with waiting until.

Until the count is cleared.

Until the bus gets here.

Until you hear your name or jail number called.

"3499922147"

Until they open your cell.

Until they close your cell.

Until the food gets here.

Until you can shower.

Until, as a new index of time, was the hardest thing for me
to adjust to. Manhattan central booking, the first stop after the
precinct, was when *until* began and time stopped. I spent close

to twenty-four hours in the precinct holding cell until the NYPD had done whatever they needed to do to get me tattooed into the criminal justice system. Mugshots, fingerprints, DNA swabs, and endless waiting in a cell while detectives expressed their disgust for criminals like me. Some called me a piece of shit as a footnote to conversations they were having with each other. One officer made it his responsibility to aim his farts into my cell. Others volunteered that I would never see the street again. They raised the volume on the TV when the news of my crime came on. Most often, though, the officers ignored me. This is what accountability for harm can look like, too. This is the form of accountability we as a society are most comfortable with, and have been conditioned to believe is repair; this is what rehabilitation looks like from the inside, and this was only day one of the 3,722 days I'd eventually serve, suffer through, and survive.

Four innocent people were shot because of me and my co-defendants. Two of those people would have no more living days to count, nor would those who survived them be able to tabulate any more days of their loved ones' life. Two died and one lost a testicle. An entire neighborhood was disrupted because of me and my co-defendants. I was attached to the worst day of some people's lives. NYC Mayor Rudy Giuliani expressed particular disgust for us animals who would venture out of our Brooklyn ghetto to shoot and kill people in Little Italy.

The day of my arrest was my initiation into a jail of another kind: guilt. At first, I was in denial of guilt. At first, I was overwhelmed with guilt. Yeah, both feelings were coexisting at the same time. I was delusional.

I was also lost. Location and space had become a dizzying abyss. After I was arraigned, I was sent back to a holding cell with twenty other men until hours later. The correctional officers, the COs, opened up the cell. A CO ordered us twenty or so men in this tiny cell to follow him. I didn't know where I was going or what was to happen next.

After two or three days of being shuffled from holding cell to holding cell I asked a Black woman CO, "Where am I? Is this Rikers?"

"No, this is The Tombs."

I had never heard of a place called The Tombs, so her answer confused me more. It would be a couple of days before I understood that The Tombs was a nickname for the Manhattan Detention Complex, known as MDC, and that Rikers Island was somewhere in Queens, but I kept this not knowingness to myself. I didn't dare ask another person where The Tombs was located. Days later when I got my first phone call I remember asking my sister, "Where am I?" Kels was an uncontrollable crier and she didn't hold back her laments when she realized that I had no idea where I was. The lawyer had told my family where I was being detained, but no one told me. That was one of the scariest feelings in the world. Several days earlier I had been free and going to school; now I was in a jail without any idea of where my body was located.

My first housing unit was 9 South PC. My booking and case number was 3499922147. I didn't know what PC stood for; or what commissary was; or that you should wear slippers in the shower; or that breakfast was served around 5 a.m. every morning; or that I could ask for a blanket to stay warm. The only thing I knew was that I should trust no one. Be skeptical of everyone. Talk as little as possible. Reveal as little information as possible about me or where I'm from. Don't get raped again. Don't talk to anyone about my case. Never fall asleep outside my cell. Don't show emotion. Biggie Smalls had his ten crack commandments to live by, and I had my own set of rules for survival.

About two or three weeks later the CO in charge of our housing unit yelled out, "Peterson visit."

I was sitting on a chair in the area of the housing unit's TV, always in the back so I could see everyone. I didn't respond when he called me because I didn't know what he meant. I didn't know people could visit me, and I had no clue where the visits took place. I was unaware of when I could receive visits. He called my name again, and this time another incarcerated guy said to me, "Yo, you Peterson, right? You got a visit. Go to the police desk." Another part of the jail lexicon I didn't know. COs were called police in jail. Even officers called each other police. Most COs held a mild animosity toward police, so I guess they embraced *police* as a term of endearment like Black people who call each other nigga.

I hadn't showered in the two or three weeks I'd been incarcerated because...I don't know. Maybe I was scared of the prison stories of people getting raped in the shower. Maybe I didn't think about showering because all I wanted to do was be in my cell where I could cry, sleep, tremble, and pray to Jehovah to get me out of my nightmare.

So when I was finally escorted to the visiting room I was ashy and stinky. I hadn't eaten more than a few apples and pieces of rocklike bread with butter in those first couple of weeks, so I was skinnier than I was at my arrest. I was in a deep, deep depression. I was in a jail inside a jail.

Because I was in PC, which months later I heard stood for protective custody, my visit was separated from the general population of the jail. Protective custody, I would learn, was the most embarrassing place to be housed in jail because it meant that you couldn't survive in general population. It was also where they housed people with high-profile crimes, and my case was in every paper from the *New York Times* to the *Trinidad and Tobago Guardian*. None of what people thought about PC mattered to me even after I found out what it meant. Jail was jail. Period. And those one-hour visits in jail, whether in PC or general population, were one-hour visits in jail. We were all in cages. Even then I knew that there was no such thing as a good cage.

I spent my first one-hour visit with my father and my brother's girlfriend, Cassiah. I was hoping to see my mother, but she didn't come. Daddy said she wasn't ready to see me in jail. Mommy had lost a lot of weight in the weeks after my arrest and was deeply depressed. She was still in shock from the crime and arrest. I guess she was taking time for herself, and I didn't fault her one bit for it. She couldn't protect me. She couldn't save me. She couldn't even see me. She was locked off from me.

Daddy, the Jehovah's Witness, the congregation elder, the head of his household, was crushed. To him, he not only failed me, but he let Jehovah down. He questioned whether he was a good father. I had kept so much of my life away from them, and it bothered him that he didn't do more to keep me out of trouble. He retired early from his job because he started having heart problems not too long after my arrest.

Prison is truly a family affair. When I went to jail the other five people in my household were locked up with me. I love those people so much. They did the time with me.

And they were doing everything they could to help me. During the visit Daddy told me that Mikey, Kels, and Mommy pooled their money together to hire a private lawyer, a Black dude originally from Compton, in Los Angeles. He was a jittery fella just like me when I got super nervous, except his voice quivered.

Fighting back tears, I pleaded with Daddy, "When are you gonna get me out of here?"

"We're doing what we can. The lawyer supposed to be good. We had two recommendations for a lawyer. The best one was a white Jew guy who everyone say is really good, and the man we get for you. We can't afford the first guy."

"Is he going to get me bail? Daddy, I wanna come home."

"Son," his voice choked from the tears he was trying to hold, "we are doing all we can to get you out. I wish I could do more. I feel powerless to help you. I don't know what else to do. You gotta pray to Jehovah. Lean on him. I left a Bible and two *Watchtower* magazines in a package for you. They say you could pick it up when de visit done."

His next words fucked me up. Now crying, he said, "Marlo, we doing all we can. I need you to learn to be a man in here."

I didn't hear anything after that sentence, so if he tried to tell me what he meant by that, with instructions on how to do this becoming a man thing, I missed it. Those words irritated the nerves of my spine. I felt disabled from parental protection in a way that felt permanent. Daddy was telling me that I needed to learn to make better decisions. I couldn't hide from this like I did with the rape and the gunshot. Facing life in prison became real to me in that moment, and so did dying in jail, and not from old age, but in a fight. I had to learn how to survive without help. That is what I understood Daddy's "learn to be a man in here" to mean. Daddy was telling me that he could not save, support, or secure me. This was the first time I realized how much I depended on his presence in my life; Mommy's, Kelly's, and Mikey's, too. I had no fallback plan, no nothing. I was alone. In jail. And no one had the power to save me.

I had to grow up fast, again. The first time was when I was violated by that broken man at fourteen, and five years later the possibility of living the life of a free nineteen- or twenty-year-old was gone. The luxury of youthful living was lost.

After the sixty-minute visit, still scared and confused, I picked up Daddy's package of the Bible, the two *Watchtower*s, and a *SLAM* basketball magazine, returned to my cell, and began reading the magazines. On my first visit to the commissary I bought a yellow legal pad along with snacks to eat. That's when I started writing to myself. I started all entries with "Dear Journal." I wrote about what I read; what I wished I was doing; about Dev, about steelpan; about not wanting a girlfriend while in jail; about getting arrested three months before graduating from Apex; about friends not visiting me; about Amadou Diallo and the cops who killed him; about Jehovah.

My writing became the place I ran to when I had good and bad news. It became my best conversant. It held my secrets, which was an improvement from keeping everything inside.

The other place I expressed my emotions was on the basketball court during my daily one-hour rec. Rec was in the rooftop cage of The Tombs. The rec period wasn't mandatory by the jail, but I made it mandatory for me. Whether it was raining, snowing, or below freezing I went to the roof to play basketball. Lots of times I'd be the only one from my housing unit to go because it was too cold, rainy, or snowy for everyone else. I'd read *SLAM* magazines and practice moves that were described in the articles and interviews. I even got a letter to the editor published in one of the *SLAM* issues.

When I did have competition I played like my freedom depended on giving my best to every game. I was a very aggressive player who had grown-man strength when it came to basketball. The strength probably came from not masturbating for the first three years of my bid. My understanding of Biblical teachings, through my rekindling with the Jehovah's Witness religion, was that masturbation was a sin. Some Scripture said that an old Jewish dude wasted his semen on the ground and that God looked down upon that. Jerking off was wrong and I did not want to piss off Jehovah because, well, you gotta fear God and give him glory. Some Scripture said that, too.

The CO who regularly worked 9 South PC, a thirty-something Black woman named Ms. Roma, took notice of my commitment to going to rec. She was a basketball fan like me. One day, as I was milling around the housing unit as I often did to clear my head or to feel busy, Ms. Roma stopped me when I went by her desk.

"Peterson, you don't look like you belong here."

"I don't," I responded, then continued milling. I wanted to say more than two words, but at that point she was just another CO, and my no-trust policy included everybody. My bid was more complicated than just the time I was facing. Even though I was the last person out of the five who were arrested, rumor was that I snitched on the shooters. I had paperwork that showed otherwise. Two of my four co-defendants were manipulated into making incriminating statements about my involvement; some truth, some lie. All that mattered to me was that we were all facing the same amount of time. They told on me. What was done was done.

But the rumor mill in jail is more potent than a high school lunchroom. Jail is a miserable place filled with people living through miserable situations, miserable guilt, miserable abuse, and miserable shame. It was hard not to want bad things to happen to people who were just as irrelevant as you. I think most people beat that urge, but those who didn't kept bleeding their hurt on others. My first real threat came several years after I was sentenced. .

Ms. Roma soon became a friend of mine. She treated me like a younger brother. She'd sneak boxes of Frosted Flakes from the officers' cafeteria to me. I'd talk to her about Dev, who was becoming a prominent basketball player in Brooklyn. She'd brag about her Portland Trailblazers being better than the Kobe and Shaq's Lakers, and she'd talk trash about my NY Knicks.

Ms. Roma did a good job of being one of the *good officers* that news pundits like to tout as examples of typical law enforcement officers. Truth was, Ms. Roma could have gotten fired for giving me boxes of Frosted Flakes if she'd been caught by her superiors. Her kindness to me came at a risk to her livelihood.

I got my first jail job because of Ms. Roma. There weren't many things to do in 9 South. Either you were a porter, a food handler, or a suicide prevention aid, an SPA. I got the job of SPA. My duty was to make sure no one tried to kill themselves in their cell at night. The perk to this job was I got to be out of my cell in the overnight hours while everyone was locked in their cells. One night I saved the life of this dude, Wes. He was about six foot two and two hundred thirty pounds, and he was having an epileptic seizure in his cell one night. I heard him lightly knock on his cell.

"Yo, Marlon, tell the police I'm not feeling well. I need to go to the clinic."

I heard him fall as I walked toward the CO's desk on the opposite end of the cell block. I ran back to the cell, saw him on the floor convulsing, yelled to Ms. Roma's fill-in to open Wes's cell. They controlled the cell doors from a station right outside the unit. The COs looked into the unit from behind a large window.

"CO, open fourteen cell now. He on the floor!"

I ran into the cell as soon as the sliding door opened, lifted Wes's head up off the concrete floor while his convulsions were taking him under the metal cot. His seizure slowed, then stopped just as the medical staff got to the unit. He stayed in the medical unit overnight and returned to 9 South the next afternoon.

"Heya Marlon, good looking out last night, bruh." Short and sweet. I appreciated every one of those eight words because I felt visible.

Near the end of my year at MDC I caught a bad flu. Jail is not the place to be when you feel weak from the flu. You have to care for yourself with limited resources. I stayed in my cell for days, only coming out to use the phone three times a day. One of these bedridden days Ms. Roma poked her head into my cell and asked me how I was feeling.

"I know there's not much I can do for you, but I hope you get better soon." Her gesture was one of the memories I wrote about in my journal.

I needed those moments to cope with the invisibility of the court process. My new Compton lawyer convinced me that asking for bail would be useless because of the severity of the crime. No judge would give a murder suspect bail. It didn't matter that I was the murder suspect, the hurt kid who was now the suspected superpredator.

Without bail, I went back and forth to court from MDC, then from Queens House of Detention (QDC), for almost three years.

One of those many court dates was on September 11, 2001.

CHAPTER SEVEN
9/11

Jail was hell.

Jay-Z's album, *The Blueprint*, was supposed to be released on September 11, 2001. It was also one of my many court dates. The department of correction (DOC) had early morning buses that cattled people from jails to court. I hated going to court. Those were the days I had the least control over my life. The CO cracked my cell open around 4:30 a.m. to give me time to get ready. About an hour later, those of us with court dates were escorted to intake cells. Some days it was packed, some days it would be just me. This September morning was packed. Around 7 a.m., the DOC bus came and we were shackled from wrist to ankle, just like all court dates. Shuffling to the bus, it was the old Negro spiritual "Wading in the Water," ashy knuckles, sleep in our eyes, uncertainty in our hearts, and freedom on our minds.

Because I was in protective custody I was usually separated into a cage within the caged bus. I was cuffed, from waist to ankle, in a cell inside the bus. I had no physical control over myself, and that was somehow protective custody. I was more afraid of what jail had the potential to do to my mind than what another guy in jail might do to me physically. Recovery from a knife wound or fistfight was easier than rehabbing a coiled mind. I thought about physical death way too much before I was twenty-five. I didn't start thinking about mental death until jail. I don't know if it was intuition, but very early in my incarceration I figured out that the thing I had to protect the most was my mind, and my emotions. The latter can have post-prison side effects. Too much emotional protection can evolve into a stifling of the heart. I didn't want people to know where I was from; my birthday; the music I liked; the television shows that made me laugh; or that I had smoked weed and drank alcohol since I was about fourteen. I didn't want handshakes or pounds from any- and everyone. I didn't want people to know I was scared, irate, happy, confused, hungry, sick, or in need of help. I wanted nothingness from everyone. My understanding of learning to be a man meant depending on myself for everything, and if I couldn't get what I needed by myself I did not get it.

In my cage within a cage, our route was from Queens House to Rikers Island, to pick up more people, and from there to the New York Supreme Court in Manhattan. Protective custody always put me on display, and I hated being in these cages within cages. But I figured out that staying in protective custody would make it difficult for me to be sent to Rikers Island because one of my co-defendants was in PC there and the judge in our case ordered that we never be housed together. Shit, this worked for me because it was easier for me to get visits in Manhattan or Queens than The Island, because the bus that took visitors over the bridge to The Island could take hours. MDC and QDC were a subway ride away. Staying in PC was a convenience for my family to see me, so for that I accepted the constant seclusion from the general population. That was the NYC Department of Correction's way of protecting my body but not my mind while I was in their custody. Even so, people got stabbed and cut in PC. COs beat the shit out of people in PC, too. Jail was jail, but this particular day everything was different.

HOT 97's morning show was playing on the bus radio as we were parked on The Island. The hosts of the radio show, Star and Buc Wild, were Black shock jocks who made the type of crass jokes that made you laugh then chastise yourself for laughing.

Star announced, "We got word that a plane crashed into one of the Twin Towers."

I thought he was joking.

A few weeks earlier, Star and Buc Wild had aired a comedy skit of Aaliyah's plane crashing. They'd aired it a few days after she'd died in the crash. I'd laughed and then chastised myself for laughing. So when he said a plane crashed into one of the Towers I shrugged it off as Star being Star.

A few minutes later he came back with another announcement.

"A second plane flew into the other Tower."

Still no reaction from me. The conversations and monologue of the other forty or so men on the bus ranged from "Oh, shit, don't we gotta drive down there?" to "What if that shit really happened?" to "Nigga, the Air Force would shoot that shit out of the air before it could hit a building in NYC."

After a few more minutes I started seeing emergency vehicles on The Island mobilizing, and COs started listening to their walkie-talkies with concern. Star came back to the radio, "A plane flew into the side of the Pentagon in Washington, DC."

To my right I could see smoke emanating from Manhattan. I started thinking about death again. Silently praying, I was begging not to die in this cage within a cage. I felt worthless. I was gonna die in a bus on The Island. I expected planes to be dropping bombs, COs leaving us to save themselves. Who was gonna stop to uncut and unshackle all of us? I couldn't save myself even if I wanted to. There was no one to control the moment, no one to call to comfort, and no one to comfort me as the news starting coming in that people were seen jumping out of the windows of the Towers.

Then I remembered that Daddy was supposed to be at my court hearing that morning. I started thinking about how I would feel if he died in the mayhem. He was to be in Manhattan that day solely for my court hearing. They said the subways were stopped all over the city. Daddy had high blood pressure.

"Suppose he caught a heart attack?" It would be my fault if that happened.

I kept silently repeating to myself, "I don't want to die on this bus. I don't want to die on this bus. I don't want to die on this bus."

My please-don't-die prayers worked. I didn't die on the bus, but I had no way of finding out about my father. The bus driver rushed us back to Queens House where we were unshackled but locked in our cells until later that evening. I was glued to my commissary Walkman for any news. Most radio stations weren't working because signals were all screwed up. For hours, while people in the outside world were dying, praying, running, and holding each other, I was in my cell thinking about dying in jail. I wonder if that's what you can describe as losing your mind.

About twelve hours later we were let out of our cells and everyone scrambled to the television and the phone. Guys were worried about their family and friends who worked in the area of the

World Trade Center. I was worried about Daddy. There was a line to get on the phone, so I watched the replay of the two crashes and the crumbling towers, reinforcing the tragedy, and imagining the guilt I would feel if Daddy was caught in the wreckage.

I guess those silent prayers worked. Daddy was safe and sound at home. He was on his way to court at the time of the crash. When he exited the train station in lower Manhattan he was directed by police to get back on the train and go home. The planes had just hit the Towers, so Daddy was able to get back to Brooklyn on the subway before the buildings came down.

My court date was postponed until January or February of the next year. The prosecutor had offered me plea deals for forty years, then twenty-five, then fifteen, then thirty-five over the thirty-one months of my remand. In the months after 9/11, my two co-defendants who had been caught running out of the bakery, were found guilty. One lost his case and was sentenced to fifty years. The second pleaded guilty in exchange for forty-five years to life. The third pleaded guilty for seventeen and a half years to life.

There were two of us left to be found guilty or not guilty, myself and the driver. As we waited to find out what was going to happen to us, I continued my regimen of Bible reading, studying *SLAM*, playing basketball, and journaling. I finally started working out, too. In the earlier days of my incarceration I had the idea that there was a physically stereotypical prison dude. He got diesel from lifting weights. When most people think about jail they think about men being raped and men lifting weights. I bought into the same story, so at first I never worked out, at least not outside my cell. I did my push-ups in my cell. Working out was also a communal activity in the jail, because rec was one hour and the weights were limited and usually broken. Unlike basketball, there was more conversation in working out, and I avoided unnecessary conversations. I remember this Latino guy name Hector, who was also facing life for murder. He pulled me to the side one day and said, "Yo, niggas here think you crazy. You don't talk to nobody except for when you go crazy playing basketball."

"Yeah, that's what they think? I'm not crazy, I just don't talk when I don't need to." Religion—my religion—was the only thing I was willing to speak about for any length of time.

I've seen no place more religious than jail. You will find the most devout Muslims, Catholics, Christians, and Five Percenters. And I had become a committed Jehovah's Witness by this time, two years into the bid. I had read the entire Bible once during that time and kept a Scripture journal, and they couldn't publish *Watchtower* and *Awake!* magazines fast enough to keep up with the speed with which I would read and dissect them. I started using court visits as opportunities to preach to others about God's Kingdom, as I had done when I was a kid with my pops in my little suit with a briefcase. One of my co-defendants was one of the people I would talk to about the Bible when we had court dates. Though we were court ordered never to be in the same holding cell on court dates, I had no problem with being in the same cell with any of my co-defendants. Yeah, some of them snitched on me, but that didn't seem like the problem to focus on. We were all facing the same amount of time, so as long as they didn't act funny style toward me I'd keep it cool, too. I knew one or more of them were stoking rumors about me telling, but I knew they knew I didn't snitch. I forgave them. They were boys like me, in way over their heads. We all needed some grace.

As time went on I felt less restrained, which led me to start working out. My first workout crew included an Ecuadorian guy who would speak to me in Spanish while I taught him English and a Korean kid who had a temper like he always had a point to prove. Ol' Dirty Bastard of the Wu-Tang Clan had just gotten to Queens House around this time. He wasn't the first famous person that I'd shared jail with in those early years, but he was the most unfit for a place like jail. He paced back and forth on the tier all day every day, digging his nose with one hand, scratching his genitals with the other.

I should have known better when I asked him if he wanted to work out with us.

"Okay, Ol' Dirty will work out with y'all today, but I don't know how strong I am." He always spoke about himself in the third person.

On day one of him working out with us he didn't last five minutes. We started him off with light weights. He dropped them faster than he picked them up.

"Dirty can't fuck with this shit." His first workout was his last.

Over the months, we were housed across from each other. He was jumped and had piss thrown in his cell by another guy, and he busted that same piss-thrower in the face with a phone receiver while the guy slept in his cell. He never showered, and he repeatedly accused people of speaking nasty about him. He was paranoid. He was mentally ill. Prison wasn't the place for him. Prison isn't the place for anyone, but for people like Ol' Dirty, incarceration is a crime against them. Jail preys on broken minds.

I witnessed and felt so many mental injuries over the rest of the bid, like the time COs rushed to search inside my mouth after I kissed my mother goodbye on her cheek at the end of a visit. They didn't wait for Mommy to leave the visiting room when they invaded my mouth. She saw it all. Of course they said, "I'm sorry, ma'am," to her, but the damage had already been done. Or the time when COs brought dogs into the housing unit to search for drugs. The dogs walked in and sniffed my cot sheets, broke my Walkman, bit into my journals, and found nothing. The COs didn't say sorry to me. They said, "Clean this shit up."

At no point did I expect jail to be good to me, but I wasn't prepared for COs to be especially malicious. It was sport to so many of them. I understood them, which is why I always kept a healthy distance from most of them. They were in prison along with us. Though they got a paycheck and excellent benefits, they were subjected to being the keepers of people who were at their worst points in life. Many were convinced that their role was to break us for the betterment of society. Only a minority of the COs understood that placing their foot on our necks took a toll on their sanity; that prison was the foot, and being an accessory to that oppression was neither necessary nor even beneficial to anyone, especially society.

In May 2002, the prosecutor offered me a twelve-year sentence. I reluctantly accepted. It was hard to accept that I should spend all those years in prison for not actually shooting anyone. But in life you get to make your choices; you don't get to choose your consequences.

My attorney, a Compton success story, said of me at sentencing:

It's a shame that youth is wasted on the young. The American dream is a dream that if you work harder, you do your school work, you're disciplined, you enter a profession, you can raise a family, you can be rewarded, and you can move up. It's perplexing and it is a conundrum why we were not able to sell that dream to Marlon Peterson; someone who was the valedictorian of PS 138, someone who has numerous certificates of merit throughout his academic years of schooling. You've heard Mr. Peterson. He is clean-cut, well-spoken, well-mannered, and he didn't get trial-ready to do those things in the two years [of his detainment]. He's been that way all his life. And yet we could not sell the American dream to him. That is frightening to me. But in the end, it's a question that we as a society have to answer. I am proud of Mr. Peterson, though, that even in this moment that we could not sell him that American dream, that it's possible that we can resell him that dream.

The only reason I remember the speech is because I have the transcript of it. What I do recall is seeing Mommy, Daddy, Kelly, Mikey, and Devon looking at me with wet eyelids. I remember deep and audible sighs from my cousins who were there, staring at me. I remember high school friends shaking their heads in frustration. I saw everyone looking at me in deep disappointment. I felt lifted and scolded at once. My actions had brought all of these people together to witness a bad day.

I couldn't relate to that American dream speech by my attorney. When did the American dream ever factor into my life? When?

I never believed in an American dream. I don't think anyone ever tried selling it to me. That product—the American dream—is a lemon. The words of the Declaration of Independence, that "all men are created equal," are a lie by omission. All men did not include Black boys like me. Created equal excluded all women. These lies are what prevent us from changing the wrongs we commit. America harms and sells the lie of the American dream to everyone, including those of us not incorporated in the framing of this nation—women, people who are Black, Brown. America's inability and unwillingness to acknowledge its first lie—the American dream—prevents it from creating a new nation, a new document that is inclusive of the humanity of everyone.

The truth is that I am not, have never been, an American monster, but the lie I told myself was that I wasn't capable of committing and condoning monstrous acts as a boy, and as a man. You have to be fully aware of your capabilities—good and bad—to understand your power to create a better self-image. Am I capable of murder? Yes. Am I capable of rape? Yes. Have I done either? No. But men have been doing both throughout human history, and I want to interrupt that inclination to follow what is normal to men. My awareness is the utility to not act out my worst possibilities. To not repeat history. To no longer follow the path of toxic masculinity and to instead live a life unaddicted to man shit. Man shit got me into prison. The belief that there was a standard to manhood that I was unable to meet as a fourteen-year-old kid, and several times as a teenager, landed me in prison. Iconizing toughness was my end. Yet toughness is what was required of me to survive in prison, so I wouldn't be someone's gay for the stay, maytag, or the victim of a CO's boredom. As much as I needed to feel vulnerable, toughness was what was needed. Still, I became more skillful while in prison in finding ways not to reproduce a kind of harm that was often a by-product of the masculine notions of muscular strength. Writing and teaching became the healthy ways in which I showed some levels of vulnerability, the spaces where I offered up precisely measured truths of my life with others.

America, I decided, could keep its dishonest dream. In that way I vowed to be un-American. I vowed at that sentencing that I would be the best version of myself for me and my community. I promised to live my dreams every day. I committed myself to making better decisions. I was twenty-two years old, and I was growing into the man Daddy tearfully implored me to be during that first visit.

My words at my May 22, 2002, sentencing were:

First thing I'd like to talk about is the incident that happened on that date, October 13, 1999. I liken it to what happened on 9/11 in that, no it didn't affect the whole world, but it did affect a whole neighborhood. And I mean, innocent people think twice about going to work and earning a living for themselves and their family. Innocent people were injured as well as killed that day...

To everyone in this courtroom, I won't allow this environment, this experience, nor jail to harden me; to turn me into a criminal, with desensitized values and morals; to build a reservoir of resentment toward anyone. I vow that prior to my arrest I was always a productive person. Since I've been in here I've been productive, and as long as I'm here I'll be productive, and when I'm back outside I'll be taking a position as a productive member of society. As I give you this vow this day, if I fail you, I fail everyone that cares for me. I fail everyone I've mentioned this to in this courtroom. I will have failed myself. I

will have failed myself as a man. And if I fail myself as a man, I
wouldn't be worthy to live.

I honor every word I said that day, even though my views on manhood and what being a man means have since evolved. Being productive won't prevent Black boys like lil' Marlon from going to jail, not really. I was trying, the best way I knew how, to make the people closest to me proud of me again. I discerned, at twenty-two years old, that individual actions impact community, and I wanted to participate in my community in a way that made them proud, too. Manhood and maleness had nothing to do with it, but I knew what I knew, and now I know what I know.

Three weeks later, on the same June day in 2002 that John Gotti died, I was transferred to state prison to finish out the rest of my twelve-year sentence. I would be about thirty years old upon release, counting the thirty-one months served, because in New York State we needed to do at least 85 percent of our determinate sentence. So as long as I didn't get more time for some prison shit, I would have to do ten years total.

The hardest part of accepting that time was knowing that I would miss Dev's teenage years. I was scared that he would follow in my footsteps. I needed him to make better decisions than me. He looked up to me and I had let him down. I taught him about the birds and the bees; how to play basketball; how to talk to a girl. All the things I wished my brother had done with me. I had broken my promise to God that I would be the best uncle to Dev, and I had to sit in that disappointment.

My next stop was to become 02A3172.

As a prisoner in the New York State Department of Correctional Services my new name became Department Identification

Number (DIN) 02A3172. The 02 represents the year that I was transferred from the city jail (Queens House) to state prison. The A represents the reception facility that I was sent to from Rikers Island (Downstate). The 3172 is the sequence in which I was processed in that year. I was inmate 3,172, processed at Downstate Correctional Facility in 2002. This "new name" was meant to force an individual to shed their identity to conform to the world of state prison. Along with that new name we had to shave our heads and facial hair, delouse, and shower in front of COs. Finally, we were given our new prison greens, our uniforms. In the years that followed I learned that this process was passed down through white history. This reception process, or breaking down exercises, are what kidnappers did at the slave castles in Ghana before the African women and men were shipped to the Americas. Iterations of this process happened again when the human cargo landed in the New World, and when they were sold to new owners. Centuries later, being convicted of a crime subjected me to the same inhumane process as my stolen ancestors, this time in the name of public safety and justice. I wonder if there could ever exist a reiteration of concentration camps, even in its most benign form, in the name of justice?

Several weeks after receiving the identity of this new me that prison wanted to create, I was transferred to the first state prison I would call home, even in my dreams. Green Haven maximum security prison is in Dutchess County, upstate New York. Looking into the infamous yard from the long, cold, ominous halls, it looked everything like a Hollywood depiction of a prison yard. It seemed like people were separated by race; you could hear the loud clanging of pig iron barbells, and the accompanying grunts from the men doing the weight clanging. Men were showering in open-air stalls. This was a different world, and I'd be lying if I didn't feel a little intimidated. And I mean "a little." This was July 2002. I had already spent almost three years in the city jail and seen fights, stabbings, cuttings, and COs assaulting the incarcerated. I was desensitized to danger, but not oblivious to it. I was becoming someone who was adjusting to the inhumanity of confinement. The location of all my dreams were in prison. When I dreamt about family, they were in prison with me. When I nocturnal-emissioned to old girlfriends they were in the cages with me. Even when I dreamt about being free, somehow I experienced that freedom inside the prison. I had become so fully committed to prison survival that I couldn't imagine living outside of it—even in the subconscious of my dreams. So when people ask me how I made it through prison, I always refer back to when Daddy told me that I needed to learn how to become a man during that first jail visit. For me, part of becoming a man meant suppressing any feelings or emotions that could compromise my safety and my sanity.

Most guys inside kept in touch with girlfriends or got friends on the outside to connect them with women they could write to, flirt with, and get visits from. I didn't want that type of relationship, even in my early twenties, when it's most natural to want intimacy with a woman. Having a girlfriend or wife in prison meant worrying about things I had no control over. I saw the pain of too many men who expected visits from a woman who didn't show up, or who didn't write them letters, or accept their phone calls. Those frustrations would manifest itself in fights and drug escapism, and I needed none of that drama. My only job, as I saw it, was to not stay in prison one day longer than my sentence, and I saw women as a distraction to my occupation. I believed that the possibility of love, of companionship, was an obstacle to free-dom. This belief system, the need to control, though of good use for me while in prison, would haunt me for years after my release.

One of the many things I couldn't control in prison was my own movement. Less than five months after I was transferred to Green Haven I was summoned back to court in NYC.

The prosecutor in my case wanted me to snitch.

Cages were hell.

CHAPTER EIGHT

SPONGE

"I just wanna tell you that I'm gonna make
you proud of me. Just wait and see.
I love you so much!!!"
—Marlon

Prison was hell.

Newbies to Green Haven had to double-bunk in a cell for up to six months, or until a single cell opened up. People were shipped throughout the NYS DOCCS (New York State Department of Corrections and Community Supervision) like Black people at a New Orleans slave auction, so cells became available relatively often. I was no longer in protective custody and I was relieved by that. PC offered no visiting perks in state prison. All the prisons were hours away from Brooklyn. I had three different "bunkies" during my double-bunk period. Light, Shaquan, and Merciful were their names. Light was about my age and on his first bid, and had about the same time to do as me. We occupied our countless hours with each other, when we weren't burning tightly folded tissue to block out the other's shit smell, by playing cards. He tried teaching me poker and I tried learning. We weren't compatible. Without cause or warning, after a couple of weeks I was transferred to another cell to share with Shaquan. He was a short brother whose DIN began with 86. He had been in prison since I was seven, and here I was, a twenty-three-year-old man who had been through so much in the past ten years.

Meeting men who had been incarcerated since the 1960s, '70s, and '80s was one of the things about prison that blew my mind. I mean, Shaquan was in prison before Mandela came home in 1990; he was in prison before 1988, that golden year of hip-hop that so many rappers rhyme about. So many lives were on pause while the world was playing. That frightened me. My life, like Shaquan's, was somewhat stalled from the point of view of the rest of the world. Babies were being born, wars were happening, new technology was being created, and we were figuring out survival and sanity behind bars while waiting for letters and hoping for hugs from anyone who knew us beyond our prison numbers.

It was Shaquan who schooled me on starving as a reasonable trade-off for the worst of the COs. The prison rule "disobeying a direct order" is the heartbeat of soul-broken COs. Because I was slow getting out of my cell one morning for breakfast, one CO, a short and pudgy white man with a thick brown mustache who could be a hillbilly reject, ordered me to give him my prison ID card.

"Why, officer? I didn't do anything."

"Inmate Peterson, I asked you to give me your ID card. Are you disobeying a direct order?"

See, this is what I call a false choice. A lose-lose for me. If I gave him my ID without him writing a disciplinary ticket, I could get an infraction from another officer for not having my ID on my person. So anytime I was out of my cell I would be at risk for getting a ticket for not having my ID. But if I didn't give him my ID, I would get an infraction for disobeying a direct order.

I gave him my ID.

"Next time you'll move your ass faster out of that cell when it opens," he said into the air in front of him.

I told Shaquan about it when I got back to the cell.

"Youngblood, you gotta hold that down. He just gone burn you a couple meals. He gone give your ID back. His punk ass just wanna feel good about himself. It's part of the bid. I got tuna fish here if you get hungry."

"I don't eat tuna."

"Aight, get you some p and j."

"I don't eat that either."

"You fucked then."

The *Saturday Night Live* reject prevented me from eating three meals until he returned my ID.

I was okay, and after a couple of weeks and without reason or notice, I was moved into a cell with Merciful. We became good friends.

A couple of years older than me, Merciful was an off and on Five Percenter, the Nation of Gods and Earths. Merciful and I had been sent upstate on the same day and transferred to Green Haven on the same bus. He reminded me of a stocky and grittier Mahershala Ali with a full head of hair. I was new to state prison, he wasn't. He played chess and I played chess. We were compatible.

The Nation was a Black Nationalist group that was an offshoot of the Nation of Islam, well known in hoods throughout NYC during the '70s, '80s, and to a lesser degree the 1990s. They believed that Black people were the original peoples of the human species, and they adhered to mathematical explanations for human thought and practice. The men were called Gods and the women, Earth. White people were called devils. The Wu-Tang Clan is pretty much a Five Percenters rap group. No doubt, the Five Percenters were a complicated bunch, and so is the religious fervor of any faith polluted with that part of maleness that is committed to harming women—asymptomatically or otherwise. Don't single out the worst parts of Black men from the worst parts of all men. The brute parts of Black Nationalism and pride are capable of transformation.

It was during my time in that cell, on the annual September 13 silent commemoration, that I learned about the Attica Rebellion of 1971. Incarcerated men died during that rebellion. Everyone wore their state green outfits from head to toe to the mess hall for all three meals, said no words, and took no food. It was probably my first experience of solidarity among people, and it felt powerful.

Two months later, a CO came to my cell to tell me to pack up my belongings because I was headed to court in NYC.

"Officer, why am I going to court?"

"I don't know. I just got a paper here that says I gotta get you ready to get on a bus back to NYC for court. You got any open cases, or an appeal on the books?"

"Nah, I don't have either."

"Then you're gonna find out when you get there. Take these two draft bags and pack up. You're gonna go sometime today or tomorrow."

Moments of power are short-lived in prison.

Merciful had no clues for me either.

Two days later I was on a bus back to NYC. Back to The Island.

I was half hoping that I was being brought back down to be released. Maybe the DA had changed her mind and didn't think I should do so much time. Prison taught me to love imagination no matter how far off it appeared. Imagination was my hope.

That hope was trampled when I got to the Manhattan court building. The district attorney was the person who had requested I return to NYC. I was escorted on foot to her office across the street from the court building. That two-minute walk with hand-cuffs felt more freeing than anything I had experienced in three years. I was walking on the same concrete with free people. I crossed a street. I saw the red DON'T WALK sign blinking, and it applied to me…and my detective escorts. It was a brisk and sunny late November day. The loss of freedom can make you ap-preciate this sort of brief moment in time. I reluctantly accredit prison with that much. It compelled me to value my desperation for freedom, for the hope of it.

Away from the stimulus of the streets I was ushered to an of-fice with several prosecutors, and the two detectives who were my personal escorts to the impromptu meeting. They got right to the point. My co-defendant, the alleged driver, was close to begin-ning trial, and they wanted me to testify against him. I can't lie, the possibility that they would want me to snitch in exchange for a lesser sentence passed through my mind, and I thought about the benefits of taking a deal like that. I could maybe be home before Devon graduated from high school. And why not? This co-defendant made statements against me that got me arrested. Telling on him would be get back.

Turned out that my thoughts were just that, my thoughts. They weren't offering me a deal. She said something to try to convince me that it would be unfair if the last guy, the driver, got acquitted, while the rest of us were already upstate. The other lookout had taken a plea of seventeen and a half years to life. Four out of five of us were done, and the driver was the last man standing. The DA wanted me to testify because, in her eyes, it was the right thing to do. I was in no position to decide what was fair or not fair for my co-defendant. Though I wanted to face the more difficult decision of whether to testify in exchange for a lighter sentence, I also felt that my conviction was the only thing I should concern myself with. I wasn't a district attorney. It wasn't my responsibility to give evidence. Four of us were already sentenced, and though no amount of convictions could balance the weight of the loss of life, safety, and health of the people harmed, I was responsible for my own actions.

I told them no. They escorted me back through the street with the red DON'T WALK sign that changed to a white WALK. A couple of days later I was sent back to Green Haven, to a single cell of my own. Several months later Kels told me on a phone call that the driver was acquitted at trial. I wouldn't want jail for my worst enemy, and I didn't view the driver as anything other than a scared Black boy like I was. He was in over his head just like me. I prayed that he got his life back together after the three years on The Island. At one of our court dates I remember him telling me that he was on antidepressants and had gotten into several fights. I never saw or heard from him again, even to this day, and I still hope for his well-being.

Back upstate in my very own cell I decorated it with my favorite quotes, including:

Therefore we do not give up, but even if the man we are outside is wasting away, certainly the man we are inside is being renewed from day to day. For though the tribulation is momentary and light, it works out for us a glory that is of more and more surpassing greatness and is everlasting; while we keep our eyes, not on the things seen, but on the things unseen. For the things seen are temporary, but the things unseen are everlasting. (2 Corinthians 4:16–18, New World Translation)

Before I was sentenced, I had read the Bible from cover to cover twice. I kept a journal of Scriptures that had a special impact on me, like that 2 Corinthians quote. Green Haven had a group of about ten or eleven Jehovah's Witnesses who met regularly in the religious services area. In a prison with over two thousand people, we were a tiny bunch. No one could accuse me of joining a group for protection.

The brothers there soon became my first community inside. All older than me, and some with as much as twenty-five years in already, they were the first group of people I allowed myself to trust in prison. Gerard, a clean-cut, bald-headed Haitian American, one year older than me in age and about ten years my senior in wisdom, especially in Bible knowledge, became the first member of the group I bonded with. I developed a love for pull-ups because he was so nice on the bar. Gerard, a father of a young girl, was serving a life sentence. He understood shorthand, and he kept a scrap book of his favorite Bible quotes written in that style. Gerard became my Bible study conductor. Several days a week we would meet in the yard to study the Bible, just like Jehovah's Witnesses did in the street. We also participated in field service in the yard. Yup, we got the latest *Watchtower* and *Awake!* magazines sent to us to preach to the other men in the yard. We prayed together and cooked food for each other from our cells. We man-hugged with brotherly love each time we greeted.

No one felt happier about my prodigal return to the religion than Daddy. He brought me the latest Jehovah's Witness publications every visit. He told me about talks he was giving in his congregation, and I would tell him about mine. I imagined coming home to the old congregation and giving talks in front of Daddy. He would report my progress to his friends in his congregation in Brooklyn. He was proud of me in a spiritual way; in a way that Mommy was also pleased about. She was relieved that I was staying out of trouble and was around people who were also avoiding making their sentence longer.

My letters to friends like Zoop and Rell included Bible Scriptures. I eventually had several Bible studies of my own that I was conducting with men in the facility. I got Bible-based books that allowed me to research the Latin and Hebrew Aramaic etymology of Bible verses. I fasted to Jehovah on the birthdays of my immediate family members, on my birthday, and on the day of my crime, October 13.

I still played basketball, but I would sacrifice ball playing time for Bible study and preaching. I was committed to my spirituality.

The more I studied, the more questions I had and the more doubts I developed about the religion. The first time I was set for baptism I decided to stay in my cell because the idea of committing my life to the religion amid my questions didn't feel right with me. Despite those doubts I was baptized on my second try in July of 2004, inside a portable tub filled with warm water in front of my congregation of brothers. I chose to suppress my contention that the God of love killed innocent kids and elderly people during his wars against places like Sodom and Gomorrah. Even if there were so-called wicked people doing vile things in those places, how could we justify the killing of the children by the hands of a loving God? How could He? I know this might sound sacrilegious to some and frivolous to others, but that's how my mind works. I have a hard time committing wholeheartedly to anything that doesn't fully sit well with me. I went along with the baptism because I thought I'd disappoint Daddy if I didn't go through with it. That's how much I loved my father.

I felt disgusted for making such a serious decision against my own conscience. I spoke to Gerard about my feelings, and he, like Daddy, gave me the "trust in Jehovah" advice. It was around this time that I joined a men's empowerment group in the prison that was disguised as a youth assistance program discussion workshop. It was here that I met Moses.

Moses, a fifty-something-year-old man, was a devout Five Percenter from the Bronx. He wore glasses, would gesture using shadow boxing moves mid-conversation, and used words with the fluidity of a college professor. He was also on his umpteenth prison jail bid. I got to know Moses through a mutual friend who knew I had an interest in working with young people after I got released and returned home. At the time I had no idea how I would work with kids, or whether I'd be allowed to since I had a conviction for a violent felony, but it was an idea that I spoke about with acquaintances. Getting word of my interests, Moses invited me to attend a Youth Assistance Program (YAP) meeting. He said school groups came into the prison on occasion and this group met to prepare for those groups.

Until that point in my bid I did not intellectually engage with anything other than Jehovah's Witness readings or meetings. I believed that the teachings of the "world," meaning secular books and the like, served no real benefit. They could only draw me away from my relationship with Jehovah. My relationship with God is what I believed had protected me from the worst of prison—the concentrated violence. I was fearful of losing God's protection and was intentional about not doing anything that could place me in His disfavor.

This, however, was a group for a youth program, and though I was having doubts about my religion, a meeting about kids was no threat to my faith.

Except that when I got to the meeting room the blackboard had "Men's Empowerment" written as the title, followed in outline form with words like Black woman, family, economic development, African history, dealing with anger, showing emotions, and manhood. The room was packed with mostly Black men, with a handful of Latinos. Moses was the lead facilitator, and he was assisted by another brother named Brother Raheem. I think he was Nation of Islam in his day job, but he, like all the men who had both religious and gang affiliations, showed no separation in speech or gesture. Round-robin style, the men debated, offered advice, educated. The only rules were no profanity, no N-word, one mic. This was no youth program preparation workshop.

And I loved it. As in most spaces, I was one of the youngest men in the room. I don't recall adding much to the conversation that first day, but I definitely wanted to come back. An older guy gave me the book, *Nile Valley Contributions to Civilization* by Anthony T. Browder, and that blew my mind. Guys threw around names like bell hooks and Audre Lorde as if it was common knowledge. It was during these discussions that I first heard anyone speak about African people before slavery. It was the first time I heard men articulate the trauma we pass on to little boys when we tell them, "Boys don't cry." The first time I felt intellectually aroused in a way that religion could not offer. I was in awe of the way Moses facilitated the conversations. He used humor to interrupt and correct. He paid attention to everyone's words, or so he made it look. I wanted to get nice like him.

A couple of months into the program Moses was transferred to another prison, because that's what happens in the penitentiary. People get moved without reason or warning. Friends come into your life for times, reasons, and seasons, then leave abruptly. The group slowly dwindled in interest and eventually disbanded several weeks after Moses left, but that group had gotten me wide open to grow outside my faith. In some ways, the answers to my doubts were being answered. I was learning from questions instead of answers.

A homie from the group lent me his copy of *The Autobiography of Malcolm X*. That life of Malcolm, his willingness to grow, even in the public eye, attracted me. His life of evolution, more than any particular aspect of his life, was, to me, his essence, his legacy. I read Sister Souljah's *The Coldest Winter Ever* in one day. Her fiction included a love story, which fed my imagination of romance and feminine contact. I satisfied my need for the tenderness of a woman's voice and feel through intoxicating romances with Jill Scott, Ashanti, and Vivian Green. I shared a passionate love with Lauryn Hill and Alicia Keys. I experienced their songs as conversations with me. I was Mos Def in the "You Don't Know My Name" video. Jill hugged me and looked deeply into my eyes in her song "Try." Lauryn and I raised children together, and we had a potent spiritual connection. Ashanti's smile warmed my soul when she said she was "Always on Time," and Vivian Green and

I had the best dates. I loved to dazzle her to blushing. There was a weekend radio station that played reggae and soca music, and I had dates for every weekend. My imagination was freedom.

These were my "club" nights. I was in my mid-twenties and wished to experience those "wild" twenties just like everyone else. I would tie one of my bedsheets across my cell bars so no one could see into my cell. I placed a green knit cap over the lamp in my room to give it the ambiance of a dull-lit club. I repurposed my shampoo bottle into a beer bottle and danced the night away with my date for the night. I created the reality I needed.

This is also how I survived prison. I imagined fun. I imagined love.

Like most twenty-five-year-olds I was growing in the understanding of myself, but under extreme circumstances. In 2004, I got my first Family Reunion Program visit. Most people understand it as a trailer visit. I had my visit with Mommy and Daddy. Yeah, most people get these visits with their wives, but the only wife I had was on a cassette tape, so I had to settle for my parents. I was ecstatic to spend two and a half days in a cabin-like building outside the prison. Though we would still be inside the prison walls, we would be far away from cells. My mother brought food to cook. She made pelau, stew chicken, macaroni pie, candied yams. They brought me Red Cheek Apple Juice. I got to see them sleep, and we got to speak without the eyes of officers. It was our first really intimate time as a family in over five years. It was balm to my psyche.

The prison also provided a Polaroid camera that we could use to take pictures of each other during the visit. All pictures were inspected at the end of the visit for anything inappropriate like nudes and pictures of the prison wall. One of the many pictures we took was one of me wearing a leather jacket that Daddy wore. It felt so good to see myself in something other than prison clothes.

Later that night I was given a disciplinary infraction for that picture. The prison accused me of taking an illegal picture by wearing civilian clothes. They gave me ninety days keeplock, rescinded my phone privileges, and took away several months of good time as a disposition. Keeplock is a step down from solitary confinement. I was locked in my cell for twenty-three hours a day, and I could go to the yard for one hour of rec at a time when no one else was outside. I couldn't go to commissary to buy food or go to the mess hall. The mess hall food was delivered to my cell. The main difference between keeplock and solitary is that I was not moved to a secluded part of the jail to serve my disciplinary time. I remained on the tier with everyone. I just couldn't interact with them.

I forced myself to eat peanut butter because it was pretty much the only food I had access to. Mess hall delivery was never in good condition, so I relied on people giving me bread to make peanut butter and jelly sandwiches.

The first three weeks were tough to adjust to. I was locked in a closet for twenty-three hours a day. There was only so much journaling, reading, and push-ups I could do in those twenty-three hours, seven days a week. But after those first twenty-one days, I shifted my brain to accept no human interaction. I took solace in reading Maya Angelou's *I Know Why the Caged Bird Sings*. She went mute for several years after a traumatic incident, so surely I could go a few months only speaking to myself. It was during this period of keeplock that I wrote a poem inspired by Angelou that would play a role in changing my life's trajectory.

Do you really want to know why the caged bird
  sings?
To maintain its sanity, that's why.
It sings to let out what it wants to hide.
The caged bird sings because of the pain it is
  constantly administered.
The bird is in dire pain, that's why.
Inhumanity, injustice, suffering.
That's why the caged bird sings.
Do you really want to know why the caged animal
  sings?
That's right, I said animal.
Repeatedly told that it is an animal.
Repeatedly treated like an animal.
Repeatedly looked upon like an animal.
Prejudged as an animal.
Spoken to like an animal, fed like an animal, made to
  live like an animal.
That gentle, exquisite, beautiful bird sings to release
  that frustration.
It sings in defiance with the words:
No matter what you think of me,
no matter how you treat me,
no matter how or what you feed me,
no matter what you do to me;
I may be a caged bird,
but I will always be a beautiful, exquisite bird.

I wrote the poem while sitting on a makeshift bucket in my cell
after the COs had denied my one-hour rec again. They weren't

punishing me more than the keeplock time, they said. They just occasionally forgot to open my cell for my one hour. Shaquan already told me that instances like this were "part of the bid." Written words were the only outlet for me to express my disagreement with being locked in a cell for twenty-four hours because someone forgot to open my cell. They were not taking my need for glimpses of freedom into consideration. They weren't seeing me. Being invisible within a cage was what I had to adjust to, and I had no power over changing the situation other than writing words that imbued my mind with resistance and beauty. Words were my place of refuge.

Eventually they reduced the keeplock time from ninety to forty-five days, and I was back to being part of general population again. I wasn't okay, but I moved on.

Months later I was transferred to Eastern Correctional Facility, with no warning, but with reason. My security classification was being lowered from the highest level maximum security to a notch lower, a max B. It was in this place that I walked closer to my purpose.

I'll never forget that day. Standing (more like shivering) in the mid-January frost of upstate New York in the yard of Eastern maximum security prison, I was on the phone with Dev, now sixteen years old. Right before our thirty-minute phone call was over he told me something that would change my life and impact the lives of many others.

"Remember Nadia from the block?"

"Yeah, how she's doing?"

"Well, she's a teacher now and she wants to get in touch with you to help her out with something."

"Something like what?"

[Operator: "You have sixty seconds left."]

"I don't know. Do you want me to give her your information so she can write to you or what?"

"Why not, give it to her. I'm not gonna hold my breath for her letter though."

[Operator: "You have fifteen seconds left."]

"All right, DJ, phone is about to cut off. I love you."

"I love…"

[phone disconnects]

To be honest, I didn't think that she would write me. Six years into my twelve-year sentence, I was accustomed to people "wanting" or "saying" that they would get in touch with me, but never doing so. I was used to disappointment; it became second nature.

Two weeks later, sitting in my ten-by-six foot cell with my bunky, a six-footish stocky guy named Lite, I was surprised when the CO dropped a letter on my cell gate and it was from Nadia. This is what it said:

Dear Marlon,

Surprise, surprise!! First and foremost, please don't think that I am lame for not writing you, if anything blame my mind and not my heart. (I ask your brother for you all the time.) I know it would have been better for me to write to you directly to check up on you, but I've been through so much since you've been away. I no longer work at Verizon, instead I teach eighth grade at the Dr. Susan S. McKinney School of the Arts; it's basically a 6–12th grade school. I love what I do, but can't stand the administration that runs the building. By July, I'll be finished with my Masters in Special Education. Okay, so now that we're all caught up I'll get down to business. Recently, I had my students watch a movie called "Redemption" starring Jamie Foxx. It was basically a movie about Stan "Tookie" Williams, founder of the Crips. It is a true story depicting his life as a gang-banger and conviction of four counts of murder. He is now on death row in San Quentin, but during his 23 years in jail he has changed his life and has written several books for school-age students to deter them from entering gangs and other lives of crime. He's been nominated for a total of four Nobel Peace Prizes, but he still faces death. My students were so moved and wrote letters to the governor to try to convince him to grant Stan Williams clemency. Now the big question would be, why am I telling you all of this? I realized that my kids have a false perception of life. They come from the Fort Greene and Farragut projects which surround the school and they think jail is only associated with those who are the worse of the worse. I found myself on several occasions telling my students about you and how you ended up incarcerated. I also tell them about another friend who was serving time because of the strict Rockefeller drug laws in New York. They've asked about what type of person you are, how do you feel about the time you're serving, and why do things like this happen. I've tried in my own way to answer them, but I know you are the one who could best answer them. I apologize for sharing your story with some of my classes without your permission, but I've been compelled to let them know that even good people are condemned for other people's actions. Perhaps being at this school is to be the voice for you to share your story. I love those kids like they are my own, even when they piss me off. But I want the best for them. With all that said, I wanted to present you with a community service project. I would love for you to send me a letter that I could read to my kids in which you tell them in your own words how you ended up there, what you've been through, your goals, and any words of wisdom that you could share with them—if that's cool with you, no pressure! Thereafter, they'll send you correspondence via mail. I'll keep a running record of the outreach you do with them so that if you need a character letter I can use this as a basis. I pray that you continue to gain strength and wisdom.

Miss you, love, & respect,
Nadia

By this time I barely engaged in the routines of the Jehovah's Witnesses. Eastern had a strong group of brothers who met regularly also, but I wasn't attracted to that type of learning anymore. So deciding to accept Nadia's community service project was a no-brainer. It did take a little time, however, for me to calm down enough to respond. I was so excited that you would've thought that I had received my release papers in the mail. Anxiety had me feeling dizzy, and tons of questions were running laps around my brain. What was I going to say (uh...write)? How long should the letter be? Words of wisdom? Who was I to be giving words of wisdom? What do I need to say to affect and infect them the most? As these questions and many others jockeyed in my head for answers, I was above all else humbled and amazed that someone (1) thought enough about me to speak to their class about me in a way that wasn't solely negative and (2) would reach one hundred miles upstate, behind prison walls and stereotypes, to seek out a guy to mentor a group of pubescent students. I wasn't

Tookie, "Hurricane" Carter, Malcolm X, or Mumia Abu-Jamal. What was so significant about me? I was only twenty-five years old, why would they listen to me?

After about three days of contemplation, I pulled out my dinosaur-age Smith Corona Wordsmith typewriter from under my cot and wrote my first letter to the scholars. I included my Caged Bird poem written while in keeplock. I didn't fully understand it yet, but I know I wanted my most honest words to inspire other people.

Mr. Marlon Peterson
Eastern Correctional Facility
Box 338
Napanoch, NY 12458-0338
February 12, 2005

Dear Ms. Lopéz's Class,

Before I introduce myself I want you all to appreciate how much of a caring teacher you are blessed to have in Ms. Lopéz. What she is doing by reaching out to me goes far beyond her paycheck. She is one of those teachers that you will remember years from now, *believe me.*

My name is Marlon Peterson, I am 25 years of age, born and raised in Crown Heights, Brooklyn, and a proud descendant of Trinidadian parentage. The youngest of three children, I grew up with the innate need to always fit in. I was the valedictorian of my elementary school in the sixth grade, I wrote for the *Fort Greene News* at the age of 11 in a program sponsored by Spike Lee and Nike. I also wrote for my junior high school newspaper. At 15 I was granted an internship at the NYC Opera while also taking journalism classes at my high school, Martin Luther King Jr. HS. I barely graduated from HS on time, went to NYC Technical School, then made news again at the age of 19, twelve days before my 20th birthday. In October 1999 I made international news in connection with an attempted robbery and double homicide in Manhattan. Five and a half years later you hear from me behind bars. How did this happen?!

Hours into my arrest my lawyer told me that I was facing 1st degree murder twice with a minimum of 25 years to life in prison. As I sat on that floor in central booking smelling mixtures of human waste and vomit I tearfully asked myself that same question. "How did this happen?" In the weeks thereafter, my father almost died, my mother and sister were walking zombies, my brother delirious, and my 11-year-old nephew was without his best friend/uncle/big brother. How did this happen? How did I, a nerdy little kid dressing up in suits and ties knocking on doors preaching *Watchtower* and *Awake!* end up in the very place I thought, and everyone else thought, I would never end up? You know, I got a cousin who was a Crip and a close friend that I earned a scar for when I was home and I used to try my best to keep them on the straight and narrow, discouraging them from the lifestyle they were living. They never served more than a few weeks in jail. While not wishing that they were ever caught in my situation, I couldn't help to wonder how it is I'm mentoring these brothers to stay away from the nonsense and here I am putting butter on my lips because the commissary doesn't have lotion.

Initially, I was able to find an answer to that question, at least partially. The first part of the answer can be summed up in two quotes:

"Do not be misled, bad associations spoil useful habits." —1 Corinthians 15:33

and

"He that is having dealings with wise persons will become wise, but he that is having dealings with stupid ones will fare badly." —Proverbs 13:20

The other part of the answer took me a couple of weeks to answer. In one sentence, in life you do not get to choose your consequences. Interestingly, I still at times have to re-convince myself of the answers because prison life requires that you constantly reiterate things like this to yourself because insanity is always a step away.

Until next time, love & guidance.

P.S. I am on the gate waiting to hear from y'all so don't take too long. I'll tell you all a little more about me, my experiences, and observations next time. Make sure you ask me a lot of questions. Being able to communicate with you all is both a joy and a blessing to me and the other brothers in here that I talk to about you all. You all help me maintain my sanity.

About two weeks later, sitting on my cot in my cell, and Lite sitting on the top bunk listening to his Walkman, an officer dropped a nine-by-twelve manila envelope on our cell window. Lite jumped down to collect the mail because he thought the parcel was for him, and so did I. I received mail once in a while; however, Lite got mail just about every day.

Reading the envelope and with surprise on his face, Lite said wryly, "Yo, Marl, this is for you."

"Oh, yeah, I wonder who sent all of that?"

The envelope was bulky. The return address read N. López, Susan S. McKinney JHS. Like a seven-year-old at 12:01 a.m. Christmas morning, I tore the envelope open. There was a stack of loose-leaf paper in this Christmas present and the letter on top was from Nadia:

Dear Marlon,

I pray that when this letter reaches you, you are in good health and spirits. The letter [you sent] was a GREAT success (see attached). For whatever reason God has chosen this time to be the season of prosperity on both our ends. Through you I have been able to find my purpose. I felt such a rush when I shared your letter and to see my students' reaction. This brings me to a fabulous idea! Creating an outreach program that allows you the platform to speak to the youth and provide them with the wisdom you have been given. I know I sometimes go hard, but look, I'm focused. I see this vision and the man above is making it all possible—feel me. (Holla at me and let me know what you think).

Holla at your girl,
Much love,
Nadia

Included in the mail was a book about curriculum design that I later used to prepare each letter to the students like a lesson plan.

We named the correspondence the Young Scholars Program, and it ran for almost a year. I would write to up to fifty students, along with a lesson plan that she would insert into her character education Friday sessions. I walked around the jail with a net bag full of letters from the kids and my notepad to respond to their letters.

A couple of months into the Eastern stint I was transferred again, two times within the next five months, eventually landing at the state prison in Otisville. Through all the transfers Nadia and I kept working together on the Young Scholars Program. We even came close to Nadia bringing the kids up to visit the prison's *real* Youth Assistance Program, where handpicked men were prepared to share their personal stories with the scholars.

But, as prison goes, the facility canceled the trip a day before the scholars were to visit. They told me that there weren't enough officers to staff the workshop. Their answer was final. All those kids who I had built a relationship with through letter correspondence got let down. I was devastated and so was Nadia.

I wasn't okay, but I moved on. I was never sure if the scholars were okay or simply moved on from the disappointment. I've always hoped that my letters helped inspire those kids into their adult years.

This program lit a fire in me to be more active in the prison. Otisville was a facility where very few work programs were available, other than being a porter. Most days men languished in the yard and gym when they weren't sweeping or mopping the same spot that the guy before them had just cleaned. It was warehousing in its purest form. I was lucky that Moses, the man I had met in Green Haven, was transferred to Otisville before me and was working in the Transitional Services Center (TSC) of the prison. TSC was a three-phase mandatory program that prepared men for their release. There was group facilitation on topics such as career development (my favorite), social living skills, and community reintegration. Moses asked me if I wanted to work there as a facilitator because he could hook it up for me. I accepted.

I had never facilitated a group or class in my life, plus Otisville was known as the old-timers prison because most of the men there had decades in the system, serving life sentences, and were much older than me. I was intimidated, no doubt. I was twenty-five years old and *only* had five years inside. Some of the guys in the classes had multiple college degrees from when Pell Grants were still afforded to people in prison, before Bill Clinton the "first Black president" (white skin notwithstanding) snatched textbooks out of the hands of men and women who wanted to pass their time mastering college and preparing for life after prison. In 1994, the same year my life changed as a fourteen-year-old, the powers in Washington, including President Bill Clinton and Senator Joe Biden, banned incarcerated people from receiving Pell Grants that paid for college behind bars. Pell Grants for people in prison accounted for less than 1 percent of the total Pell Grant spending, but like always, people in prison weren't anything more than convicts and superpredators who deserved retribution as punishment, and only empty gestures toward rehabilitation.

These classes I was to facilitate weren't like the meetings at the Kingdom Halls. The men were mandated to attend these classes based on where they were chronologically in their sentence. Phase One was for everyone entering the prison; Phase Two was for those near the last two or three years of their earliest release date; and Phase Three was for those with under a year left.

Before any facilitator got into a classroom, they received a big-ass black binder with hundreds of photocopied pages of exercises

and curriculum for each corresponding topic. We couldn't re-
move the binders from building 107 where the Transitional Services Center was located, so I took pages of the binders back to
the housing unit every night to review. It felt like high school all
over again when I'd take the textbook home to read, except this
time I cared about classwork. I was training to become a teacher
in prison at the same age of a teacher outside. I was growing up.
Most people who go to prison at a young age grow up and mature. Most people outside prison mature, too. But most people
like to believe the illusion that prison is the intervention that
stops crime. But no, it's getting older, having a sense of usefulness,
believing in something you want to live for.

Nadia and the kids in her school, along with my co-facilitators
at TSC , Moses, Bourne, Chinese Lee, Ché, Big Tom, Rakim,
Boo, Serious Black, old man 'Bama Newton, Reem, and the hundreds of men who I would eventually facilitate classes for over
the next four years were the community that grew me. They were
my accountability, my intervention. Except for Nadia and the
Young Scholars Program, all my teachers were crooks, murderers,
arsonists, heroin addicts, drug dealers, and recidivists. They were
baldheaded, Black, Latinx, Chinese, Indigenous, Garifuna, face-
scarred, fathers, sons, husbands, grandfathers, great grandfathers,
Ronald Reagan Republicans, Assata Shakur loyalists, *Wall Street
Journal* enthusiasts, and immigrants. We were a medley of people
who were usually insecure and rarely certain. We were a community of healers, warriors, jesters, and teachers. We were people
broken by experiences, surviving the best way we knew how. We
were you.

That's the thing about prison that I wish more people understood. Incarceration doesn't rehabilitate; people do.

Most of the lessons in there were out of touch with what the men were dealing with and felt more like standardized pre- and post-test lesson plans. The more skilled facilitators like Moses and Bourne researched their own material from the jail library and had their loved ones send them books and related reading materials.

Observing those guys teach also sparked a feeling that there was so much I could learn from trying new things. That's probably why the word *precedent* stood out to me. I remember reading it in a book and thinking that it was a typo for president. When I looked it up, the words *model*, *pattern*, and *example* got my attention. The skill set of Moses was a precedent that I wanted to follow, and I viscerally felt the need to try new things to be of good use to others.

Bourne helped me get to where I needed to be. Bourne and I shared a birthday, but he was ten years older. He chain-smoked Top tobacco, did everything with a chip on his shoulder, and played basketball with a heart that made you forget his scrawny stature. He coached me into facilitating my first class. He helped me prepare notes, and like Moses he modeled using your personality to put the classroom of usually disgruntled men at ease. He used to call me his little big brother and Young Semi. Semi was Arsenio Hall's character in *Coming to America*. I guess he was Eddie Murphy, the king.

Bourne had an edge to him that most people did not like. He and Moses barely tolerated each other. More than once I had to play mediator between them. The fluctuating group of eight to eleven facilitators debated endlessly about everything.

The Transitional Services Center was its own building, and as facilitators we had two classrooms that we used as offices where we prepared for classes. Each office had a radio that we left on 98.7 KISS FM, and the office had one rule that applied to everyone who entered: You had to do your best two-step dance. I think it was my friend Serious Black who came up with that.

Serious Black earned his name. He didn't joke around with anyone, except with me. Black was serving about seventeen years into a fifteen-to-life sentence when we met in Otisville. I remember seeing him tear up when I shared some of the Young Scholars letters with him. His tinted glasses and cornrows were a well-manicured disguise for a man who always spoke about creating programs for the elderly once he got out. A member of the Moorish Science Temple of America, Black was one of the men I missed the most when I left prison. A leader in his own right, he never missed an opportunity to encourage me to lead things. Moses, Bourne, and Black were some of my most influential teachers. They taught me the importance of being assertive and how to defend my opinions. They grew me from a bashful young man into a confident adult. They helped me realize that I had a responsibility and gift for inspiring people beyond children.

Nadia, who was now more than just a friend, and had become one my mentors and closest advisors, encouraged me to go for the role. She was also growing into more responsibility as an educator, and she shared her learnings with me through phone calls and visits. The Young Scholars Program ended because she went on to an elevated role in an all-girls school, and the girls' needs at that school were different from the kids in Fort Greene. Despite the end of that program, Nadia would become one the people closest to me. She opened me up to the idea that I could have a positive impact outside of jail. Nadia was an angel to me during this time and season, and I loved her for it. It felt as if she had been brought to me to reveal my possibilities.

When Spank, the man who pretty much ran the Transitional Services Center, was paroled after serving twenty-seven years, the other guys, my elders, suggested I take his spot as the de facto head of the TSC. The real authority of the TSC was Matt Rose, a counselor employed by the prison. He was a balding middle-aged white man, legally blind, and Republican. His favorite words were, "Always do the right thing," and he bragged about his wife of thirty years being the only woman he slept with. He still used the wallet his wife gifted him decades earlier. Matt loved to give big hugs and was never shy about tearing up when the emotion came. To us he was one of the cool ones. To his colleagues he was an inmate lover. Matt became my accomplice as our relationship grew, but that did not happen overnight.

Matt didn't trust me in the beginning. He had been working with Spank for years as they came up with programming for the TSC. They were around the same age and I was half their age, and reclusive. Matt wasn't eager to have me in Spank's position, which included helping men retrieve important documents prior to release, such as their driver's abstracts, birth certificates, social security cards, rap sheets, and letters of support from reentry organizations. The official title was administrative assistant, and in that role I wasn't expected to facilitate classes anymore.

Begrudgingly, Matt promoted me into the position, though I had no aspirations of being another Spank. I realized that I liked facilitating classes. The feeling of sharing information and encouraging men to hope beyond the moment was a high for me.

Around this time I started a college correspondence program for an associate's degree in criminal justice. The prison didn't offer college so I had to pay for the course from monies in my commissary account. I'd send them about $30 a month to keep the work coming. It was what I could afford. I figured I'd pay the whole thing off after I got out and got a job.

The correspondence classes introduced me to terms like corporate culture and organizational development. I began infusing what I was learning in my courses into the TSC. I even developed a mission statement for the TSC that I printed up in banner-style lettering and stapled to the wall:

PROFESSIONALISM TRANSCENDS PRISON

This banner could have easily been remixed to read: PEOPLE IN PRISON ARE PEOPLE. TSC was work, but it was viewed as *prison work by prisoners* and that carried a subhuman connotation. Though some of the world's greatest thinkers, healers, and leaders have spent time in prison, in real time incarcerated people aren't allowed the grace of possibility and purpose. No group of people are more baptized into this belief than the incarcerated, and it makes sense. Whether you feel guilt because of the harm you've committed, or whether you are innocently convicted, those feelings, coupled with being caged and treated like an unwanted animal, can ingrain in you the idea that you are less than. I knew what I was working to overcome and I wanted everyone who walked into that room who saw the PROFESSIONALISM TRANSCENDS PRISON banner to respect our possibilities and purpose. I wanted us to believe that we could beat prison and that no one was better than us when we worked at being our best selves. We were leaders in the prison, and recognizing that, I wanted to lead us to possibility.

A new chapter in my life was germinating. I thank the Young Scholars for this. I mattered to them, which meant I could matter to others. They sparked the notion that I was more than a crook, that I had value beyond the hell of my confinement.

It is around this time that I mailed the following pink sticky note to Mommy:

I just wanna tell you that I'm gonna make you proud of me. Just wait and see.

I love you so much!!!

CHAPTER NINE

FREEISH

Prison was hell.

I hurt Mommy so much.

I know I did.

For all my talk about supporting and listening to Black women, I disrespected my mother and her home. Mommy didn't deserve losing weight; her hair falling out because of stress; the crying every day and night; the feeling of shame from neighbors and family; detectives crowding into her home before the sun rose; the violating touches by COs during visit searches; phone calls that cut her off midsentence; the insinuations from court officers that she wasn't a good mother; or her own self-guilt of not being a good enough mother to me. I was her baby, and I turned my back on everything she had sacrificed for me. Broken people break people, even those whom they love, and I broke my mother's heart.

And it gets worse. Back when I was clumsily hiding that I wasn't in control of my weed smoking, my partying, or my trauma, I was fully aware that I was hurting her—and Daddy, and Kelly, and Mikey, and Devon. The sadism was real. Every day

I walked out of my apartment I knew I could end up defending my life and that felt so overwhelming, especially because I was dealing with it all by myself. No one knew that I'd cry in prayer, asking God why he was letting all of these things happen to me. I carried my pain with grace, as I still do, but back then I had no understanding that being abused by others so deeply affected how I comported myself. Back then, the only way to protect myself, or so I thought, was to ignore hurt—mine and those of others.

Mommy did not deserve this.

Mommy to me, known as Elsa to family and friends, and Petronilla to white people, my mother is a reserved but spicy Trinidadian woman who could party better and longer than your mother. She seemed to juggle with ease waking up at 5 a.m. to travel by train and carpool to work in White Plains, cook for us when she returned home at around 7 p.m., gossip for hours on the phone with her friends, be the one to check that the front door was locked at the end of the night, party when she wanted, fend off Daddy's new and stricter religious views, and window-shop for hours in Manhattan on Saturdays with me in tow.

It is also so dope that she did whatever she wanted while caring for us. When Daddy became a Jehovah's Witness, he stopped partying, rarely drank, and cut out R-rated movies.

Fun ended.

For him.

Mommy partied, drank, and cussed. She went home to Trinidad Carnival every year after she got her green card—even playing a mas while she was pregnant with me, and lived her best life, like she should have. Playing a mas (short for masquerader) was the pinnacle of the Trinidad Carnival season. Playing a mas was borne out of resilient and creative Canboulay celebrations in

Trinidad during the island's eighteenth century French coloniza-
tion. Enslaved Africans were prohibited from the pageantry of the
French pre-Lent festivities, so our people did what we do best. We
created a better version of the French Carnival by adding drums
influenced by West African traditions. We mocked the French
bourgeoisie with our homemade costumes, the mas. These Black
people created joy through the act of rebellion. Kelly, Mikey, and
I rebelled right along with Mommy, too. While Mommy and
Mikey and Kelly were partying all over Trinidad during the Carnival season, on most days I played with kids in the area where
we stayed, which was in the Queen Street plannings in Port of
Spain—the generationally neglected government housing com-
plexes similar to the projects in Brooklyn, or to Hanover Park in
Cape Town, South Africa.

Mommy let me roam in Trinidad. I guess she felt safer and
freer in the island of her birth, and she let me enjoy some of that
freedom, too. I used to have a crush on a girl named Marlene,
and we would chase each other with suckabags dripping from

our mouths. There was my Trini road dog, Roy, who was a year or two younger than me. Roy and his family lived in the apartment directly above us. In the mornings Roy would yell my name from outside, or I would do the same to him. It was our call that it was time to roam. We ran in random staircases with slippers and sometimes without them. We flew homemade kites, rolled in dirt, picked out the cars that were "ours" as they drove up Queen Street. I played freely in those plannings. I felt braver there than at home in Brooklyn.

And though she had lived in Brooklyn longer than her years in Trinidad, Mommy never referred to America as home. She emigrated from Trinidad to the United States in 1967; got her American citizenship in the '80s; worked and earned her social security here; raised her children in America, and married her husband in the Brooklyn Borough Hall. But she has never relinquished her right to call Trinidad the only home she has ever known. You can't fault her for never feeling welcomed in America. The white and Jewish men she worked for scared her because of their sexual advances. White police scared her because she knew they would kill her or her boy children if we didn't act right. The police killed an innocent Black man named Arthur Miller three blocks away from our apartment a year before I was born. They strangled him to death, on the same block that me and my siblings and some cousins went to elementary school, PS 138. The idleness of the young Black boys in our neighborhood who were languishing on street corners made her nervous—for me. Without a formal mother-and-son lesson in civics, Mommy taught me that love for country is about more than being thankful for whatever opportunities we might have in America; it was about feeling welcomed and safe.

That's why she made sure that all of us grew up immersed in Trini culture. Our music, food, dance, Trini slang, and passed-down stories were the safe haven she created for all of us. Mommy was committed to the responsibility of passing her culture to the next generation. She took me to Trinidad for the Carnival season almost yearly, against Daddy's wishes. Arguments happened, and she always won. I don't think Daddy fully understood that his pull to religion was most valuable to his own journey, and not that of his family's, and that the two could coexist. Mommy cared that we learned "we culture."

It's really because of her that I play steelpan and go to Trinidad for Carnival almost every year. My father was the former pan player, but my mother was the cultural ambassador who fully shared her pride for being from the land of calypso and steelpan. She took me to see mas, to the j'ouvert morning street party, and to the "jump up" in a band on the road. She jokingly teased how I was gonna dance with a girl when I got old enough. Mommy taught me how to enjoy myself. Her older brother, Fitz, a high-ranking prison officer in Trinidad, sang amateur calypso in local shows called tents. They were a brother and sister tandem who blessed me with the uncageable spirit of fun. That cultural pastime of finding fun in misery, of enjoying my own company, was another way I survived prison.

Too bad, though, that I couldn't experience prison without bringing her in there with me. She did nothing to deserve living in a cage, especially a cage created by her own son.

I saw the tired in her eyes during those visits to prisons hours away from Brooklyn. My bad decisions took some of the fire out of her. Shit happened to me when I was young, but I chose to react in unhealthy ways. Even though some choices aren't good options, the alternative does exist. Clouded, cluttered, and closeted, maybe, but choice always exists.

I expected to see her on my first visit along with Daddy. When Daddy said that she was not ready to come to see me yet, I didn't react. I knew what I had done to her. I had wounded her. She needed to find the right kind of bandage to contain the rupture of my actions. She avoided unnecessary interactions with the state her entire time in America. She voted, and worked polls on Election Day, but that was the extent of her getting close to government. She worked hard to stay away from welfare and the police, because both "want to be up in yuh business."

About a month or so after I was inside she finally visited me. Her face looked exhausted and defeated. She was seated before I got to the visiting bubble. Her first glance at me was followed by a weak and frustrated shake of her head in confusion and hurt. She looked visibly smaller.

I walked up to her and we hugged, then we slowly sat down across from each other.

I could see her exercising her facial muscles to muster up the strength to ask, hesitatingly, "Are you okay?" The stories about people being raped in prison don't only traumatize the person in prison. The loved ones of the incarcerated have sleepless nights, too. They fear being harmed by the news that their brother or son or boyfriend was raped. Prison is never experienced in a vacuum. Never.

I was three months old the first time she took me with her to Trinidad Carnival. She said her father put his hat on my head at j'ouvert. She always reminded me that I looked like her younger brother Kenneth who died when they were kids. He was ten years old. And it was undeniable that my mom and I were physical twins.

It was she who the school dean called when I was robbed by those boys when I was nine, and it was she who the high school dean called when I was beaten in the hallways of George Westinghouse when I was fourteen. Mommy taught me the importance of good penmanship and good diction.

Sitting in that visiting room, we both knew that if I said I was not doing okay, or that some bad thing had happened to me, there was nothing she could do about it. We were powerless.

I told her I was okay and deflected, "Mommy, how are you?"

"Boy, not good. Not good at all. Is it true that you were a part of this thing?"

My lawyer had warned me not to speak to anyone about the details of the crime, including my family, because anything I said could be used against me in my case. Being under that embargo was the perfect excuse to not have to tell her the truth to her face. I wasn't ready to accept accountability for the harm I had caused her. I had taken away her freedom when I fumbled mine.

"The lawyer said I shouldn't talk to anyone about my case, not even you."

I cannot imagine what it feels like to know your child could go away to prison for life without knowing if they were deserving of the fate they were facing. I can't imagine what it feels like to have your son or partner go to work and hear that they were killed at their job by a group of kids. Nothing about being the person named defendant, perpetrator, accomplice, inmate, or convict can take away the guilt of knowing that I played a part in taking away the freedom of others to live out their existence.

Over the years, the visits and the guilt became more routine than eventful, and the weight of my decisions blended into Mommy's body more organically. The rupture was bandaged, but I don't think it ever fully healed. Mommy couldn't protect me from the air I breathed, or from the ways I allowed my wounds to bleed onto her. But she held a job as a home health aide, did most of the shopping for the prison care packages I received, managed a husband who judged her for not becoming a Jehovah's Witness, and hid the shame of her son, the one child who is her physical twin, inmate 02A3172.

There was no mask to hide the stench of living in a poor Black neighborhood. Most people survive the poisons of street violence, police brutality, underemployment, and rampant drug misuse, but there are those of us who don't make it out without causing severe damage or becoming severely damaged ourselves. The scar tissue I grew also impacted Mommy, and my father, who is now growing into vascular dementia.

My bad for skipping into the present, but Daddy is aging without memory. Remembrances of the past are things I wish would grow out of my memory. Sometimes he forgets that I went to prison. Sometimes I wish I didn't remember. Most times I remember too much. As Daddy's memories dissipate and morph into disjointed moments in time I hope he still remembers, even if in fragments, that he is another reason I survived prison. I will never forget that.

For the first two and a half years of my incarceration, he visited me every single Friday, and when he couldn't make it he would arrange for someone, a friend, someone from the Kingdom Hall, or a relative to come in his place. Even when he sent a replacement, Fridays were *our* days. I was learning about him and he about me.

Those Friday visits were a different sort of air for me. They began in a transparent bubble with space to fit about four kindergarten-sized tables for visitors. From there we moved to Queens House, where we shared the dance floor with everyone, no protective custody to general population separation. It felt more like community. Queens House would be my home for two years. For sixty minutes this man would listen to me talk about basketball, the Bible, jail politics, and new words I learned. For that hour, he spoke about his teenage years, old girlfriends, his relationship with Elsa before she became Mommy, the Bible, prayer, and his steelpan mentor, Anthony Roc Williams. We spoke about Kobe. We spoke about Alicia Keys.

Daddy attended every court date, brought me the latest *SLAM* and *GQ* magazines, along with the *Watchtower* and *Awake!* joints. He kissed me on my cheek at the beginning and end of every visit. He hugged me closely every week. Close enough to where I could smell his Daddy scent. He was a breath of fresh air.

Daddy taught me about loyalty and compassion. He would say to me, "Marlon, it is my priority to visit you every Friday. Everything else comes second." I don't know if I should have felt good or bad about that, but I know they were words I needed to hear. I was a sensitive kid whose greatest fear was being seen. I wasn't naturally tough. Visibility ran synonymous with being exposed for my sensitive inclinations. People robbed, beat, and raped me when I was visible. Shame pushed me to hide within. Hiding within meant I had to create a mask that others could see so I wouldn't be faceless. But Daddy saw me. He was the chief judge of the family, but jail changed him, too. His son had shocked his system. The nine-year-old boy who was giving speeches became a nineteen-year-old crook.

I think he accepted my situation before I did. I think he convinced himself that he had failed me as a father. Jail confuses the shit out of everyone who comes in contact with it. Despite that confusion, Daddy came to see me every week. You gotta understand why that meant so much to me. I was so scared every day, not from any physical harm, but from the idea that people saw me as disposable. Every time I went to court, every time a CO made me bend at the hip, every time I read the autopsy report of how the innocent souls were shot, every time the cells closed at 11:30 at night, every time they opened around 5:30 for breakfast, every moment of every day all I could see was that the world didn't want me to exist. And despite all of that he wanted to see me. Every week.

He was my life, and he didn't deserve to see me so broken.

But, after that one hour of being seen by the love of my life, I'd switch back to being aight. Prison required my full attention.

You gotta understand that I saw my father as my first king. I likened him to the physical representation of Jehovah. He wasn't my God, but he was my first teacher. Before my teenage years he was the person who I spent the most time with. He taught me how to read, how to ride a bike, how to speak in public, and how to show care for people I didn't know. Some of those valuable lessons were relayed during our walks to and from the Kingdom Hall or in field service. Sometimes they were late at night in the bedroom when everyone else was watching television.

I remember his excitement the day I gave my first speech in the Kingdom Hall. After my mini-sermon the older brothers and sisters in the congregation took their turns congratulating me, for the talk, and him, for raising a boy like me. In those moments of gratitude, speaking about Jehovah, the God of my religion, and being taught about this religion from my father, I believed in him almost as much as I believed in *Him*.

But that's the thing. No amount of love or attention from my parents could have saved me from myself and the way the elements of my experiences surrounded me. I was broken before I was an adult and I lived it out with inconspicuous grace.

But, I was still *okay*.

Over the years of my sentence the routinization of guilt, loneliness, and rapid self-deprecation dwarfed the constant threat of violence. I developed a dermis that desensitized me to seeing COs beating men for talking too loudly on the way to the mess hall, and those of my own kind cutting and stabbing each other over the prison version of the free market. Owing someone too many stamps cost a young brother his life in Green Haven. Cigarette and gambling debts got a man stabbed at least a dozen times in the yard. I remember being in mid-conversation with someone when the violence began, and continuing the conversation when the stabbing ended. On another occasion I was watching a re-run of *Girlfriends* on BET in the yard with an old-timer named Carter. About two feet in front of us a Latino gentleman walked behind another Latino man and slit his face with a razor from the left corner of his mouth to the left side of his neck. The culprit walked away. The victim let out a hot and low grunt, held the fall of his face now hanging from the cut, and went looking for a weapon with urgency, but inconspicuously. Carter and I went back to ogling over Tracee Ellis Ross and company. The COs in the yard didn't recognize anything had happened until the victim began chasing the guy who he wanted to become his victim. Even then, what was happening on *Girlfriends* was more interesting than what was happening in the place that we lived.

None of that is okay, but it was a necessity for me to survive. It was a way of maintaining sanity. To allow every harm to bother me would be counterproductive. I had to learn to expect pain of the highest kind, and that expectation was an acceptance of my circumstances. That was being productive. I had four responsibilities while in prison: Don't do anything that would make life any harder on my family. Don't do anything to extend my sentence. Learn as much as I can about everything. Survive. In that order.

I never thought about healing. I was okay.

CHAPTER TEN

BRIDGING THE GAP

> *"If you had more than a week left to go I would ship*
> *you out of here and lose you in the system."*
> —Sargent Shayborn

Prison was hell.

White people never enamored me, but I was curious about them. I was learning about Black people before slavery, and I guess I wanted to understand why they were the way they were.

What made them believe they were great leaders? So I'd borrow and read from the prison library books like Hillary Clinton's *Living History*, Tom Brokaw's *The Greatest Generation*, and Rudy Giuliani's *Leadership Through the Ages*, among others. They didn't talk about bell, Audre, or the Nile Valley Civilization. They spoke about Black people, but not in a way that they saw anyone outside of a nonviolent "I Have a Dream" Martin Luther King as relevant or powerful, or justifiably violent. They loved Martin as a holiday, not the extremist for justice. They loved Mandela, but not Madiba. Black people were compressed to civil rights issues.

Growing up, there were sprinkles of white men called Bethelites who were regular congregants at the Kingdom Hall I went to as a kid. Not all Bethelites were white or men, but the white ones were assigned to majority Black and Brown communities. That was how I saw it back then. And now. But it was all love with the Bethelites.

The Bethelites were Jehovah's Witnesses who took an oath to be domestic missionaries within the various congregations. They dedicated their services to Jehovah by living communally in the central branch of the religion based in Brooklyn. In the best part, too. The Brooklyn Heights Promenade has always been my favorite part of my borough. The Manhattan skyscrapers slicing clouds as they pass, the East River presumptuously bridging to bordering boroughs, and the Brooklyn, Manhattan, and Williamsburg Bridges all within view—it's my kind of urban paradise. It is busy, bold, and beautiful, and this is where the global center of Jehovah's Witnesses was located. This is where the Bethelites took us Kingdom Hall kids to play in the park. I had nothing but good memories about those excursions.

The white brothers were my first real interaction with white people. I always assumed that they lived in big suburban houses before they volunteered their life, or a few parts of it, to live on a stipend in great urban housing. I wanted to live where they lived.

But I never felt the need to be like them. I remember being a ten-year-old picking out *The Autobiography of an Ex-Coloured Man* from my library on St. Marks Avenue. No school assignment; the title interested me. I read *Black Like Me* in the seventh grade. I remember being frustrated with the Rodney King beating. And the verdict. That verdict.

That's when I began to stop seeing police as allies of people like me. I understood why it was important to rejoice over OJ's not guilty verdict, and it was why I embraced the killing of Yankel Rosenbaum as being justified. White people and the Orthodox Jews got away with shit we couldn't. Gavin Cato was seven years old when he was killed by a car in a three-car motorcade and left to bleed out and die in the street. The driver was a Hasidic man, Yosef Lifsh. Gavin's seven-year-old cousin, who was with him, had her leg broken in two places, her tongue cut in half, and her ear hanging from her head. No one was charged or indicted. A few years before that, Yusuf Hawkins had been beaten to death by a white mob in Bensonhurst, Brooklyn. Michael Griffith, a twenty-three-year-old man, originally from Trinidad but who lived in my neighborhood, was chased down by a white mob in Queens into an expressway. A car killed him. White people and Jewish people, who I easily conflated, were not my friends; they were killing us because we were Black, and they usually got away with it without any accountability. This was oppression, and justice under its boot is often led by justified anger, and unjustifiable violence.

So, the possibility of white friendship never appealed to me, not until Vassar College. Not until I met Larry.

I loved Larry Mamiya. He took care of me like a proud father-mentor. I don't think I ever got to tell him that. Dr. Lawrence H. Mamiya, a Hawaiian, started bringing Vassar College students into New York State prisons in 1979, beginning with Green Haven prison. After the Attica Rebellion in 1971, many of the men who were transferred to Green Haven organized themselves into the Green Haven Think Tank. These guys are the reasons why anti-violence programs in prisons exist. They are responsible for the "seven neighborhoods study," which exposed the fact that the majority of people in NYS prisons were from seven neighborhoods in NYC. At the time those neighborhoods were Bedford-Stuyvesant, Brownsville, Bushwick, East New York, South Jamaica, Queens, and South Bronx. These neighborhoods were majority Black and Brown. They were the poorest. With support from Quaker prison volunteers, the seven neighborhoods study evolved into fighting for the restoration of voting rights for formerly incarcerated people and advocacy for those still locked up.

The Think Tank also created the prerelease center as an organizing hub where incarcerated men provided peer counseling to support those facing parole board hearings and those transitioning back into society. Despite prison, these men, who included Eddie Ellis, former Black Panther and founder of the Center for NuLeadership Policy Group on Urban Solutions, conjured up and operationalized what would later become known as reentry.

Twenty-five years after Larry's inaugural class entered Green Haven in 1979, the program had expanded to several other prisons. That expansion included the state prison in Otisville, where I was confined from 2005 to 2009. After Spank's release, Moses told me that it was my job to run the Vassar program. He didn't wanna fuck with the predominantly rich white kids—his words not mine. Moses was two years older and was a long-time member of the Nation of Gods and Earths. Moses wasn't a hater of white people, but he didn't like the way white people were pedestaled, especially in prison.

I agreed with him. White guys in prison had the best paid jobs. They dominated the honor block housing units. That's the way I saw it, that though they were the minority in NYS prisons they were the most taken care of by the prison system. I don't know this to be fact, but that's what I observed during my decade behind bars. The Vassar program, at least when I was introduced to it in 2005, had this taste of privileged whiteness, and I saw an opportunity to change it up.

After a few months in my new role, Matt began trusting my abilities. He gave me space to create programming that I thought would improve the services offered to the men who shuffled through the TSC doors. The first thing I wanted to do was to return the Vassar prison program to its genesis as a peer-led program and not the model that had devolved into students coming into the classroom to ask the incarcerated men questions about their existence, without much reciprocity. The students were not smarter or more cultured than the incarcerated men, nor were the guys locked up any better than the students. I saw value in reestablishing an environment where the interchange of views, supports, and resources was prioritized over the freeness and whiteness of the Vassar students.

I felt the distance during my first interactions with the students. It was the first time I was spending significant time around white people who were close to my age group. I had never been in classrooms with white people, at least not this many all at once. They appeared uncomfortable—most of them. I'm not sure if they were uncomfortable because of us, or of just being on the inside. I had heard about them from other veteran facilitators. They said the *kids* were fun to be around, describing them as prissy rich white kids, always looking high. Honestly, I saw them as tools for narrative change. As potential accomplices for good trouble. I neglected to share my vision for them with them, though.

In 2006, Bourne and I conjured up the idea of Otisville & Vassar—Two Communities Bridging the Gap (BTG). Using the book Nadia had sent to me to create the curriculum for the Young Scholars Program, *Understanding by Design*, by Grant Wiggins and Jay McTighe, I created a twelve-week program that I called a practicum of experiential learning. The curriculum included the foundation of POP—the Power of Persistence. Included were interactive debates, mock parole board hearings, career development interviews, Tech Fridays, and most popular, Floetry Fridays, which was started by Andre Ward, a comrade who was the Otisville steward of the Nation of Islam. In these two-and-a-half-hour Friday sessions the students and the incarcerated men taught each other. We created a curriculum similar to my two-week Career Development Transitional Services class. The overarching goal was for everyone, but especially the incarcerated men, to stand in their value and self-worth. Disrupting the feeling of worthlessness was important. Fun in learning was prioritized. Being honest to self was encouraged. I made it clear that two people who always agreed with each other meant one of them was lying. What I was really doing was working out my own issues through my classes. Sometimes being selfish is being selfless.

Most of the prison men in the class filled all the statistics of the undereducated incarcerated population, but they also had a wealth of knowledge that wasn't appreciated or measured by policy makers on the same level as the knowledge of the nineteen-year-old college students from Vassar. Some guys even said it. A few internalized the illusion of inferiority, and who can blame them? Everything about prison and jail is designed to compel worthlessness. It's hard to feel whole when an officer can search your person and direct you to "Turn around. Bend over at the hip. Spread your ass cheeks. Stand up. Face me. Lift up your dick. Now your balls. Run your finger through your mouth. Open your mouth. Say 'aaaah.' Lift up your right foot. Wiggle your toes. Left foot. Wiggle your toes. Let me see your hands. Put your shit back on and head back to your housing unit." Those were the words I'd hear from a CO after every family visit. Imagine hugging your mother, son, or partner, then walking fifty feet away into a makeshift closet with a CO. They got to see parts of my body that I never saw.

Transitional Services was my distraction from worthlessness. BTG became the same thing for the other participants. We used activities and icebreakers that were originally designed by the Alternatives to Violence Project, one of the programs created by the Green Haven Think Tank and Quaker volunteers. One of my favorite exercises was the Adjective Name Game. Everyone got to pick a positive adjective that starts with the first letter in their first name. Over the years I was Marvelous Marlon, Merciful Marlon, Magnificent Marlon, and Motivating Marlon. Feeling good about yourself when you are walking with daily depressions is a revolutionary act in a cage designed to deplete. The shame of the act committed, the guilt of the conviction, the anger of the daily humiliation, the hurt of being abandoned by loved ones, the hurt of abandoning—all of it was so heavy.

But we all got by.

Some of the heaviness was performed on the first day of each new group of Vassar students. I named the exercise Reception Center. It was a lightweight simulation of the transition process for all incarcerated people from the county jail to state prison. Downstate Correctional Facility, eighty-three miles away from Brooklyn, was my reception facility. That is where we were broken in, taught to become state inmates. COs cussed and threatened us with medical attention if we didn't follow a direct order, our heads and facial hair shaved clean, sprayed for lice, and given our inmate identification number. Reception was the most isolating part of my time in prison, even worse than the forty-five days in keeplock. We ate three meals a day but on a timer. We rarely got enough time to eat the meal before we were ordered out of the mess hall. We could take four slices of white bread back to our cells. No one except the two incarcerated porters were allowed out of their cells for the first two weeks. It was a quarantine period for all new admittances to the state system to make sure we weren't coming to prison with any contagious diseases. During the COVID-19 quarantine, the Centers for Disease Control and Prevention issued guidelines for managing COVID-19 behind bars that were impossible to follow. At one point during the height of the first surge of the pandemic, forty-five federal inmates and zero staff died from the virus. Prisons are flippant with people's humanity, aren't they? They treat people like an illness or a disease. So you get why feeling good about yourself in prison is labor.

The reception center simulation was a harsh introduction for each new class, but why lie about how we felt during that jail to prison transition?

Once the students were escorted into building 107, they were asked to shut their mouths and put their hands behind their backs, "X" at the wrists. We cussed at them, yelled in their faces, ordered them into the classroom, made them face the walls. We made a student cry once. We scared straight the college students the way that TV shows like to exploit young people in the justice system. But, for us, crying wasn't an intended outcome. I apologize for that. We could have been more creative about sharing the feelings we'd had during that reception phase of incarceration, but we had to let them know that some of us held racial grudges against white people because most of the officers in reception were white. We called the students all sorts of names—cracker and redneck—when we took on the roles of COs. The cursing and name calling was all they got, and it was all that we could give them. They knew they weren't prisoners, but we manipulated their minds into believing that they were. I remember a girl crying because we instructed her to give us her sneakers. Her response was the extreme. Most of the time the students were quizzical. Their eyes were either afraid to make contact with ours, or their glances suggested they were groping for help; looks I remember feeling when I was broken-in during my reception experience at Downstate. Though we were experienced facilitators who also understood the utility of role-play in teaching, this was a risky exercise in hindsight. Thank God no one had an anxiety or panic attack.

We ended the exercise, and "broke them out" of prison with lots of smiles and laughs. Then we got down to debriefing the exercise. We set the tone for the room. We joked on each other as facilitators because we also understood the importance of creating a safe learning space *despite prison*. The first day's lesson concluded with the Adjective Name Game. Over the following weeks, the classes featured debate sessions about affirmative action, gay marriage, and rehabilitation versus redemption. We created mock parole board hearings where the students and incarcerated participants played interchangeable roles as parole commissioners and parole candidates. We rigged the decisions so that most people would be denied the opportunity for parole, which mirrored reality. In 2004, only 3 percent of people with the highest degree of felony, like A-1 felonies, were released from parole in NYS compared to 23 percent just ten years earlier, despite empirical evidence that people convicted of the most serious crimes are less likely to recidivate.

We asked everyone to dress like they were going on a job interview for our Career Day session. Both the incarcerated and the Vassar students got the chance to be interviewer and employer. Every once in a while an incarcerated student would pull me to the side and say, "These Vassar students don't have any clue about what they want to do for work." Most nineteen-year-olds, and definitely the majority of college students of that age, are clueless about their careers. The assumption that the incarcerated students disrupted was that white young adults are prepared for the adult world. Nope, they aren't any more prepared than I was at nineteen, the age of some of the Vassar students and my age at arrest. Privilege gave them a leg up for when they decided to grow up.

And we spoke about race explicitly. I had gotten my hands on *Teaching for Diversity and Social Justice*, by Maurianne Adams, Lee Anne Bell, Pat Griffin, and several other contributors, including JoAnne Silver Jones. I liked the book so much that I wrote letters to the colleges where the contributing authors taught. I was looking for mentors and thought one of them would be down to connecting with me. JoAnne was one of two contributors who wrote back and the only one who stayed in touch with me.

She became my pen pal. I appreciated her immensely when she wrote me after she was assaulted with a hammer when she visited Washington, DC, to celebrate the first Obama inauguration. I was surprised that she continued writing after she recovered from her attack. My instincts were that she would see in me the person who violently attacked her and discontinue the pen pal relationship. JoAnne and I are still buddies today.

In all the BTG sessions, I sprinkled in parts of the curricula from the book around race, class, and gender. There were definite racial elephants in the room that we could interrogate behind the prison walls. One of our Friday sessions was themed Racism and Discrimination.

BTG had gotten some buzz in the central office of the Department of Correctional Services, and they sent two administrators to sit in on this class. Matt debriefed with the two administrators. Their only critique was that an inmate was running the class. Apparently they thought the Vassar students were the ones running the classes. They thought we were less than, incapable, or unworthy of leading a class with college students. This feedback was a sign of drastic changes coming to the BTG. There was suspicion by the attending CO that Otisville students were enticing the Vassar students to like them romantically so each class was attended by two correctional staff members, Matt, and another prison counselor, Ms. Jackson, a devout Christian and middle-aged Black woman with a Southern drawl. Ms. Jackson watched over each class like a strict Pentecostal Sunday school teacher. If someone cursed during the discussion, Ms. Jackson would interrupt, "Now, we don't need to use that type of language, do we?" We all respected Ms. Jackson and usually edited our words in real time. So if we couldn't cuss in the classroom, how could anyone be enticing the college students?

But what if they were? I mean, what if there is an attraction? Platonic or romantic? Asha Bandele's memoir, *The Prisoner's Wife*, is the story of how, as a prison volunteer, Asha falls in love with Rashid, an incarcerated man. The result of that "illegal" relationship was a marriage that resulted in a book that I read twice in two days. It was a self-help book of sorts for men inside who were in relationships with partners on the outside. My friend Sheila Rule, a former *New York Times* editor, met her husband as part of a prison ministry letter-writing program through the famed Riverside Church in Manhattan. They started a company to help other incarcerated families during his twenty-five years to life sentence. Though I never had a romantic relationship with any volunteers, what if I had? I might hurt someone's feelings? They'd break my heart? People do that to one another all the time without the inconvenience of cages. No, the underlying assumption is that people inside are incorrigible and will take advantage of volunteers, manipulating them into bringing drugs or weapons inside. That's definitely a possibility, but regular visitors and COs bring contraband into prisons all the time. Lockups always have drugs inside, and most people inside are not interacting with any volunteers on a regular basis. The end result, though, is that the institutional memory of incarceration serves to remind the inmate and the volunteer that they could never be true equals, that there could not be integrity in a classroom setting.

With the Vassar students in particular, I felt the assumption was that Black and Brown prisoners were taking advantage of white girls. Most of the students were women, because Vassar College was 60 percent female. Black men are always positioned as threats to white women. True or not, that was the message I was getting, and I let the prison administration know how I felt. I typed up a letter to the superintendent of the prison articulating my grievances with the new no contact policy, because rehabilitation should never reinforce the presumption of danger or otherness.

If we really believed in Bryan Stevenson's words that no one should be defined by their worst moment, then the courtesy of grace should begin in prison, if, that is, we are committed to keeping those dungeons alive.

Visitors and volunteers weren't exempt from the prisonization. (Yeah, I be making up words and justifying incorrect grammar, just like prisons and jails make up rules.) When I got locked up I was sentenced to social isolation in a facility for a period of twelve years. Social isolation increases the risk of premature death for every race, and surprise, surprise, the risk doubles for Black people.[1] We are always dying at higher rates than white people from one thing or another, yet they are the ones always complaining about being replaced or outnumbered. That delusion shows up in America in its prisons. Incarceration is the direct result of white people believing that they needed to dehumanize everything Black in order to prosper. Prisons are built on former slave plantations in the American South. The same tactics used to break a slave are used to break an inmate. None of that prevents this nation from investing billions in an institution borne out of chattel slavery.

The Vassar students, and all volunteers, were subjected to dehumanization as soon as they entered the prison. The Vassar women in the program often complained about the way their clothes were sexualized by officers at the search area. The showing of an elbow in a T-shirt was sexually suggestive. Fitted jeans were too tight and would excite the inmates. Rules like that diminished the women into one-dimensional characters typecast as the romantic interest. Visitors were scrutinized even more.

Prison rules are set up in a way that assumes that the men inside are sexual monsters who will obsess, grope, or rape any woman who enters the facility. And sure, there could be some truth to that, assuming all men in prison are (1) heterosexual and (2) lack self-control. These rules also assume that the incarcerated men are the only people in a prison who are capable and willing to harm women. COs participate in rape culture right along with the parts of the incarcerated population who they share porn magazines with. COs are often men, and I have yet to meet a man who hasn't cosigned or fully participated in the objectification of women. People in prison are the same as people outside the lockup. The prison rules are created from the conditioning that people inside are wildings, different from the rest of society. Remember, people harm women *then* go to prison.

As Fyodor Dostoevsky, himself once incarcerated, said, "The degree of civilization in a society can be judged by entering its prisons." Prison rules make an indictment of the larger society. In women's prisons, the rape culturists wear badges. No one classifies COs as predators in the same way they do incarcerated people. Between 2009 and 2011 women were only 13 percent of the prison population, but accounted for 67 percent of staff-on-prisoner victimization.[2] Eddie Ellis, a former Black Panther, once said, "Prisons and prison populations are a reflection of what takes place outside of the prisons. The direct relationship constitutes the basis by which we propose that there are no prison problems, only community problems. Once we begin to address community problems, prison problems will also be addressed."[3] All I'm saying is that we have a societal problem of sexual violence toward women, not a prison problem of sexual violence toward women.

At one point the prison initiated a policy that the Vassar students could no longer hug or make any hand contact with the Otisville students. We were directed to speak at a distance. We could be in the same classroom, but we had to be socially distant. They did not want us to be touched. What is something like the no contact policy supposed to do to your psyche? Break you. Reaffirm your guilt. The policy was an actual rule that could be interpreted and enforced in any way the prison decided. Directive 4750 of the NYS DOCCS rules and regulations states: "During orientation, volunteers must be cautioned regarding the seriousness of personal/emotional involvement with inmates. This will include visiting, corresponding... and accepting phone calls."

The rule was a warning for volunteers to suppress the thing that makes us all human—the consciousness that we can feel. See, that's why I believe that prisons are senseless in their perceived purpose. Prisons and jails don't help people. People help themselves despite prison. And we hugged and fist-bumped the students despite the risk of being caught.

That letter to the superintendent got me summoned to the senior counselor's office and a visit from the deputy superintendent of programs. Both of them relayed the superintendent's anger with the letter and the accompanying warning that if I ever wrote her a letter again to complain about the program, she would transfer me out of the prison. The threat didn't bother me because I was under two years from release, and by that time in my bid I didn't care which prison housed me. They were all slave plantations to me. Plantations weren't the problem, slavery was. The location of the facility agitated me less than the peculiar institution of prison.

For one of the Floetry Friday sessions, where everyone shared an original talent with the class, I wrote a poem that expressed how fed up I was with being defined by my worst moment. A CO was stationed in the classroom when I read the poem. Who knew that ten years later a hoodie worn by a Black boy in Florida would become a rallying cry for Black Lives Matter.

> *Let me take my hoodie off*
> *Let me take my hoodie off.*
> *Bridging gaps*
> *See you can't stop it.*
> *See/*
> *When you sit here every week*
> *And they sit here every week*
> *And we sit here every week*
> *We become us*
> *And, see, we can never be weak.*
> *Can you dig it?*
> *Even when they portray us as a son of gun*
> *In here because of guns*
> *Intentions to leave and pick up guns*
> *Assuming we can't wait to corrupt, cajole, connive,*
> *Pollute and program their young white minds...*
> *Yea, same ol' song.*

Us—the crooks
Us—the criminals
Us—the con artists
Us—the drug dealers
Us—the murderers.
You—the rich
You—the innocent
You—the right
You—the White
Misconceptions
Wrong or right
Gaps
Bump that, we bridged that
Even though you don't want that.
Now,
We ain't all right.
Some I won't trust in the still of the night.
Without a lamp, flashlight, and God's might.
I ain't painting pictures that ain't right.
Deceiving the masses about
"It ain't fair"
"The system put me here"
"I don't deserve to be here,"
blaming everyone else for everything else
Ignoring that the answers and the blame,
the questions and the shame
Lied within self.
Gaps bridged!
See, I ain't here to preach
Just bridge

I ain't here to sneak
Just bridge
I ain't here to freak.
I ain't here to do what you expect me to do—
Which is fail.
I bridge
Just bridge.
When they claim that all we do is play?
See, that can't be true.
I've seen brother Roc cry—paroled after his 5th try.
Determined D hug a guy
Youn Anna recited and cry.
Nice Mini sigh
Outstanding Oscar raise his ever radical fists to the
*   sky*
Victorious ask for advice
Serious Black morph into Rigorous Rob
Super Steph mature before my eyes
Jazzy J inspire me to write
Diversified open up timid eyes
Courageous Chris show why he's wise
And saw Sara smile 1…2…3…
all the time.
Seen hip hop on trial before Oprah tried
Immigration
PTA meetings
Parole mockeries
Discussions on HIV.
FUN AND GAMES?
That's all you see?!

That's all you see?!
Nah, that's what you want to see.
Like Bush hunting WMDs
Moses trying to convince me that Macy Gray is sexy
Or dreaming that girl Beyoncé will be visiting me
After she dumps Jay-Z...
Hey, that could happen.
The point is:
See, what you see are the perversions within thee
Exaggerated to the highest degree
Fantasies of your inequity
Mixed with apprehension of frivolity.
Based on what?
Our impeccable record of integrity?
Our dedicated dignity?
Our desire to empower others in green.
Enlightening those still young & green;
While bringing them together with those that do
     quarterlies.
All for $13 or $14 every two weeks.
Worth the gray hairs?
Hardly.
But we do it.
Daily.
Weekly.
Monthly.
Don't compliment me.
Just respect me.
See,
When you sit here every week,

And they sit here every week
And we sit here every week
We become us despite all the dust
Despite all the fuss
The accusations and the distrust
Denials and disapprovals
Common unity is built
Bridges are built so strong—
Foundation so strong.
I'm talking titanium strong
Benching 310lbs strong.
Real love strong.
Can you dig it?
Let me put my hoodie back on.
Let me put my hoodie back on.

Nothing changed after the poem. We kept defying the rules. During the ensuing weeks the administration started hassling the students on their entry into the facility. For one of our sessions that we called Tech Friday, administration searched the dorms of all the Transitional Services facilitators and the areas where we worked in building 107. The college students took the lead on Tech Fridays. It was their job to present the latest technology to the incarcerated men. They couldn't bring in any electronics, so they pasted, wrote, and stapled internet printouts of the latest cell phones, computers, and online job search services. Through them I learned about Facebook and search engines. Lots of the Otisville guys were already up to speed because they read tech-related magazines or had family members send them their own internet printouts about technology. Their interactions as experts on any topic was no different from the conversations I've had at stuffy places like Rhodes House in Oxford, only more passionate, more informed by lived reality.

And just like the conversations I've had in privileged places like Rhodes House or Harvard, sometimes guys made homophobic comments, and sometimes the Vassar students exposed their own white privilege. Sometimes the incarcerated men reinforced negative stereotypes about masculinity and nonconsensual chivalry. Sometimes the Vassar students' fascination with the inequities of incarceration felt voyeuristic, patronizing, and informed by white guilt and pity.

No one's actions were excusable. But it happened. People challenged each other, sometimes they didn't. That's just how societies work, prisons included. Whenever you place people together you create possibilities of growth. Those Vassar students met experts

The 6th Otisville & Vassar "Two Communities Bridging the Gap" Appreciation Day December 11, 2009

"Being incarcerated has changed my outlook on the world as a whole. Bridging the Gap is about getting to know people from different perspectives and showing the world how powerful change is. We are not animals behind these walls and gates as the world depicts us. We are just a reflection of each other's potentials, and a result of each other's decisions."

BTG ALUMNI

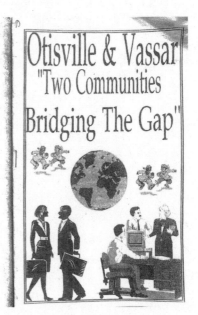

of lived experience and rigorous readers of books and human character. The incarcerated men—we—didn't need those students for our growth, but it sure helped. What mattered to me was that I was helping to create safety and inspiration in hell. I was learning as I was doing, and I was evolving into a person who felt less confined by my confinement.

CHAPTER ELEVEN

DECARCERATED

Prison was hell.

I would be lying, though, if I made the case that programs in prison were the sole reason why I was becoming freer. Dev, my nephew, was one of the main reasons why I did not become the savage that prisons want to create. He was my everything. I think he was the first person I ever fell in love with. My parents and siblings, I was born into their love, but Dev, he learned to love me and I created space for me to love him. Dev was my lifeline. I thought about him when I needed to convince myself that living was more important than dying. Dev was a comedian at heart. At the end of our visits, few and far between because he was a teenager who deserved to spend time being with his friends and not traveling hours to a prison, Dev would hug me deeply, pretend to rip off my clothes like they were rip-away sweats that basketball players wore, pat me on the butt and say, "good game." It was so funny and COs would look alarmed every time he did it.

Dev was growing into a NYC high school basketball household name as the starting point guard for one of the best high school

STATS AMORE

NY SPACE
DEVON PETERSON, Lincoln senior guard

MY VITALS
Height: 6-3
Weight: 180
Age: 18
Residence: Crown Heights
Resume: High-energy guard averaged 19.7 points, 5.4 assists and 3.6 rebounds per game in his senior season, and has upped his averages in the main statistical categories every year that he has been at Lincoln.

MY FAVORITES
Movie: He Got Game
"That movie kind of talks about and shows how my life is now. It's about a basketball player growing up in the neighborhood, trying to make it, and that's me.
TV Show: Martin
"Martin is just hilarious. When I'm feeling down, he's like the only person that I can watch to make me laugh.

Video Game: NBA Live '07
"It has good graphics and the players are able to do moves that look real. My team on it is the Miami Heat."
Dream Date: Beyonce Knowles
"She's the hottest chick in the game."
Sport (other than basketball): Soccer
"I always liked soccer because I respect the way the athletes are able to run 90 minutes up and down the field without stopping."
Food: Chicken/peas stew
"I'm West Indian, so it's a dish I've always liked."
Role Model: Uncle Marlon
"I've looked up to him since I was young because he was the first person to teach me about basketball."
Artist: Jay-Z
"He speaks about the total opposite material (of) other rappers. He talks about real stuff, and he's the greatest rapper of all time."

Song: "Warning" by Notorious B.I.G.
"I never heard any rapper tell a story like Biggie does in that song. The first time I heard it, I played it over a hundred times."

MY QUOTE ON SENIOR YEAR:
"I've been to the Garden every year since I've been at Lincoln, and to return there in my last year of school would mean a whole lot. I gotta go back. It never gets old. There's this energy I feel when I step on the Garden's court. It's such a historical place to play."

teams in the country, the Lincoln Railsplitters. At least two to three times a week his name or picture would appear in the city newspapers. Newspapers weren't easy to get inside, but the fellas inside made sure I got the paper whenever they mentioned Dev's name or included his picture in the sports section. I started collecting his newspaper clippings. I read the fifty-to-five-hundred-word sports blotters about him and his team. I kept a picture of him in his team uniform next to my pillow. When we spoke on the phone I tried to let him know that I supported him, that he made me proud, that he could be so much better than me.

I'm telling you all of this because I don't think I could have survived prison without witnessing him living a full life not following in my footsteps. I needed him to breathe free, so I could wheeze less haphazardly. During his junior year, from the dayroom in Otisville, I watched him play in the NYC PSAL High School Basketball Championship game at Madison Square Garden. Several guys watched with me, and I was nervous and anxious. It was my first time seeing him play basketball since he was about eight or nine. The deep pride I had didn't come from his prowess on the court, it came from knowing that I had not failed him. My biggest fear about being in prison was that Dev would follow me, that he would fail at being free; that he would be just like me—too scared to be himself.

He was brave. Lincoln won the championship that day. He led his team to three NYC basketball championship wins, and he was the MVP of the NYS State High School Championship game that same year, beating future NBA star Kemba Walker. In an interview with the *New York Daily News* he was asked who his role model was. "My Uncle Marlon," he said. "I've looked up to him since I was young because he was the first person to teach me about basketball."

He kept me alive. He gave me the will not to break. He was my bridge to believing that I was somebody's beautiful bird. I love Dev so much. His spirit uplifted mine from the day he was born. He was my guardian angel.

By the seventh year of my bid, as Dev was evolving into a superb ballplayer I was devolving into a less than mediocre one. I spent more time in the Transitional Services Center. The prison allowed for three program and/or recreation periods, after breakfast, after lunch, and after dinner, and I spent every period in building 107. I had started a criminal justice college program through mail correspondence, paying installments from whatever I had in my commissary account. I'm still surprised that the college took $30 a month as payment for classes. My time in 107 was spent studying for school, writing curricula for the classes I facilitated, preparing parole release packages, and writing résumés for men. Listen, I had access to a computer and a copy machine and I learned to do shit so I could help my guys out. The resources belonged to the people and the people should be able to use the resources however they wanted. And I didn't charge for nothing. It never made sense to make money off people for things I had no control in creating. Nothing in prison belonged to me, except my peace of mind. I wasn't wise enough yet to understand that all the resources in the prison did, in fact, belong to me, to all of us.

Prison programming and prison jobs can create hierarchy in the pecking order of prison status. I worked in an office and classrooms; most guys worked in the yard as porters. I can't front that it felt a little like house versus field nigger. The difference for me and the other guys who worked in Transitional Services was that we were committed to be a thorn in the side of the administration. One of us was always getting in trouble for using the copy machine to print personal and legal documents for whoever needed it; we would swipe confidential information about reentry budgeting or programs and get it out to the prison population; we used personally developed curricula in the classes where we were expected to use the prison manual. We were always trying to disrupt in our own way. When I left prison, that disruptor strategy came along with me.

The breaking of prisons requires disruptive innovation. Shake up the status quo and expose a new need for freedom. Once the new need is created the system will glitch. Innovate during the glitch. Make freedom easier.

Organizing as a means to freedom requires that you identify with a lineage. The big homie kai l. barrow, someone I'd meet years later, emphasized that in all conversations about justice and liberation you need to know the lineage of your principles. "What is the foundation of your work?" she would ask.

I looked up to Malcom X. He believed in Black possibilities. His pops was a Garveyite, and his moms was from the Caribbean. The Trinidadian in me felt like Malcolm X and I shared a tribe somewhere down the ancestral line. Maybe he had the lineage of Merikins like my family, the renegade enslaved Africans in the American South who joined the British Army during the War of 1812. After they participated in the burning of Washington, DC, they relocated to unsettled parts of Trinidad and created a self-sustaining community without white influence or interference. Was Malcolm also a Merikin, or maybe a Maroon descendant? I don't know, but there was something about his spirit that felt kindred. His oratorical skills resonated with me. He was comfortable telling white people "no," and the same treatment was reserved for Black people who were lost in whiteness. He consulted with people like Maya Angelou and Muhammad Ali. He was a hood dude. He understood what prison felt like. He understood me, and I understood him. We wanted exodus from cages. We embraced evolving in belief and perspective.

But X was dead and in books. People like Angela Davis and Eddie Ellis were alive *and in books. Angela Davis: An Autobiography* was one of the first books I read when I was sent upstate. The book was left in a cell that was my home for about a week. Strange cells with property left behind became homes quickly when time spent anywhere was so transient. Probably not too different from foster homes, a conduit to prisonlike schools.

Before that book I had never thought about women in prison. I saw them when I went to court, but I didn't connect their struggle to mine. They were superfluous and ancillary. But Davis had served time in Manhattan just like me. She survived despotic COs. She cried to herself, and she fought the inclination to be defeated by the bid. I wanted to be like her.

I wanted to be like Eddie Ellis, a thinker and former Black Panther who served twenty-five years in NYS prisons. He had cowritten a seminal work, "The Non-Traditional Approach to Criminal and Social Justice." It was scholarship about the prison experience by people who were in prison at the time. The Green Haven Think Tank had laid the groundwork for powerful possibilities beyond prison for people like me. Before we graduated from ex-cons to formerly incarcerated persons, we were developing data to understand the institutional racism that plagued our communities. We didn't need COVID-19 or the term mass incarceration to expose what we already knew—that America didn't love us.

The first time I saw Eddie Ellis was on a 2007 video of the annual Vassar–Green Haven Reunion organized by Dr. Larry Mamiya. Every year, former participants in the Vassar College's Green Haven Prison Program—formerly incarcerated students and Vassar students—got together to break bread and talk about the work they were doing for the community and their postprison release stories. I lobbied Mr. Rose to get a copy of the video so we could see it on the inside. We had a TV and a VCR in building 107, and every free moment I would rewatch the video, sometimes with other guys, but most times by myself. My giddy ass was so enthralled by the video that I organized a special viewing of the video in one of the building 107 classrooms for whoever wanted to come. That video illustrated our possibilities beyond prison. I had done time with people who were on that video, and they looked good in their street clothes. They didn't look broken.

I wanted to show as many people as possible that there was life after death.

The work of prison abolitionists like Angela Davis, Ruthie Wilson Gilmore, and kai l. barrow made this way happen. Black people made this lane happen through their resistance and creativity. They dreamt our freedom. They proved for me that my Black convict life mattered, too. Many died so that we could fight better, like the brothers in Attica, or the women in Bedford Hills who produced programming that created a safer existence for all of us while inside. Freedom fighters like Kathy Boudin and Donna Hylton paved a way for possibilities while inside. Watching those two women in the documentary *What I Want My Words to Do to You* was the inspiration behind the PROFESSIONALISM TRANSCENDS PRISON banner I created. While advocates like Eddie Ellis and Dr. Divine Pryor inspired me, the women in that video filled me up. Their personal essays about who they were before prison connected with me in a kindred way. They were doing the work of freeing themselves from their pasts—an abolition of personal guilt. In a way, the work of the women on that documentary made the idea of a world without prisons, the way Angela Davis wrote about it in *Are Prisons Obsolete?*, viable. Possible.

Abolition is a politics of creationism. Wanting to end policing is wanting to create thriving communities that do not need an armed state security force that has no true legislative and judicial accountability. A world without prisons is the manifestation of solutions to socioeconomic problems. A world without prisons is a root-reckoning of the community problems that preface the prison problems that men like Eddie Ellis and Larry White asserted in "The Non-Traditional Approach to Criminal and Social Justice."

Abolition is wanting to live without fear. Have police succeeded in establishing societies of safety? Have prisons? Has parole? Probation? Deportation? No.

No.

No.

No

And, no.

But I get why abolition seems impractical to many, and un-
sustainable to others. Fear. Asking people to imagine an America without mass incarceration? That would mean that there was
never a government policy and law enforcement directive to im-
plement a War on Drugs. Working backward, no War on Drugs
would mean that there was no Jim Crow, redlining, or mass
lynching of Black people. No Jim Crow would have to mean that
slavery of Black people never happened, which would mean that
mass kidnapping of Africans would not have happened, which
means that the story of American ingenuity embedded in the myth-
ical American dream would never have happened. Abolition
means the undoing of America, not just the mere unraveling that
happened in 2020.

No wonder it scares people.

George Floyd's eight minutes of American martyrdom fame
interrupted the comfort of the American facade, but it wasn't
enough to prevent more than seventy million people from voting
in solidarity for a white supremacist sympathizer as president...
of the free world. His racist, sexist, deceptive, and megalomaniac
habits were not enough for people to partake in a fucking solidarity vote against him and his unsettling tweets that cause international hypervigilance. Big George's eight minutes and forty-six
seconds was not enough for a quick arrest of the cops who killed

Breonna Taylor. The family, and their supporters, wanted the arrest of her killers as justice in their eyes. Oprah, Beyoncé, a whole-ass new organization called Until Freedom, mass protests for months, a *Saturday Night Live* performance from Megan Thee Stallion, a Louisville state of emergency declaration, a $12 million wrongful death lawsuit win for Breonna's family, global pressure from allies in the Caribbean, Africa, Europe, could not get expedited justice for Breonna's family. The president-elect couldn't do it.

But we got BLACK LIVES MATTER painted on streets across the world. Don't misconstrue what I'm saying here. The imagery of the words of three homies I know, three Black sistas, will live in history with the phrases "I have a Dream," "Black Power," and "Amandla." Black Lives Matter is legend. But, the family of Breonna wanted an expedited arrest, no different from anyone who makes a criminal complaint. It was the least that could be done after Big Floyd's eight minutes and forty-six seconds of involuntary American martyrdom. But, we got words painted in the streets.

America's refusal to listen to what Black people ask, plead, strategize, and demand is the core of the American sickness. Justice is undoing all that is needed to acquire redemption from brokenness. More than seventy million people decided against a simple act of solidarity of firing a man whose presidency unmasked the truth of America: that it is a brittle republic that depends on lies to survive.

And Black Lives Matter*ing* is a way out for America—a road to redemption. Abolition is a route to restoration. Being un-American is the undoing necessary to create anew. See, when Breonna was executed; when Big George cried for his mother; when activists demanded the reallocation of police budgets to community resident resources, America only heard *defund American deceptions*. Instead, they took a knee with protesters.

That's not what people in the streets requested. They—we—want less policing, not because our communities are trouble free, but because policing is a part of the trouble. Policing has always been part of the American brokenness, even before cell phones, even before camcorders, even before Malcolm, even before Ida B. Wells. We want America to stop policing us because policing is synonymous with our death by mistake, by malpractice, or by intention—it's always our death. Abolishing policing is a proclamation that we can do bad by ourselves. It is also an exclamation that we can create better communities if police give up some of that money that is spent killing us by mistake, by malpractice, or by intention. The doing away of policing is a doing away with the need to be policed by armed people. But, America believes in armaments more than it believes in its lies of white racial superiority, more than the possibilities of the people here, more than it believes in life, liberty, and the pursuit of happiness. And in my experience, people cling to weapons when they are scared. I don't know if I live in a terrified nation, but I know that this nation is terrified of people who look like me, which makes people like me terrified of this nation. All of this fear suffocates space for love. Love for others makes you want to undo behaviors that hurt.

Until that undoing occurs, abolition will remain an impractical ideal for America. But this ideal is a powerful organizing tool for all of us who understand that creating a new nation under God and indivisible requires an undoing of the old America to which we pledge allegiance. One way or the other, prisons will become obsolete. The American founding is also the story of the abolitionists' struggle against British oppressors. The hardest thing to do is to believe you can run away from your past. At some point history repeats itself, but with different oppressors and different abolitionists.

I became a prison abolitionist out of necessity and because I wanted to create new possibilities for men like me inside.

Then I met this guy.

He walked up to me when I finished my set on the pull-up bar in the yard on a sunny Sunday morning. Bill and I had talked trash in prison basketball tournament games. That was the extent of our interactions in Otisville. That Sunday morning he wanted to learn more about the Young Scholars Program that Nadia and I started together. Word had gotten around the prison about the program because I shared the experiences of the young people with my classes; I'd even ask for their advice on how to respond to some of the problems the kids mentioned in their letters. Bill wanted to be a part of it in some way. Nadia and I had ended the program by this time, but I took him up on his ask.

We met up in the yard later in the week, and I told him about the genesis of the program, the books I used to design curricula, and the idea of character education, all shit I learned through the books that Nadia sent to me. Bill was an eager-ass dude. He wanted to team up to start our own letter correspondence program from prison. And you know what? I don't remember ever hesitating to say yes. I'll let him tell his side of those first interactions when he publishes one of the thirteen or so books he wrote in prison. He was serving a twelve and a half to twenty-five years to life sentence for a homicide, which meant he was eligible for release after he served twelve years and six months, but could be denied parole release for up to twenty-five years. He was committed to writing a book for every year he served. He almost completed that personal vow, too, after serving thirteen and a half of those years.

He and I began meeting every Thursday night during rec time in a room adjacent to the prison gym, named the Blue Room because the entire place was painted blue. The engineer that he is, he recruited Spud, Butta Lab, Shaq, and Malik to help build out the idea. All of us were serving sentences for violent offenses. I don't think it was Bill's idea to recruit them because of their offenses. He picked them because all of them had spoken to him about helping young people, and, in his eyes, this was their chance. During one of our Blue Room strategy meetings, Butta Lab and Malik came up with the name How Our Lives Link Altogether—HOLLA.

None of us came from the same neighborhood, we were all serving different sentences, and we had different religious affiliations. I had known Butta Lab from Green Haven. A well-known Muslim who came up with people like Afrika Bambaataa, Butta Lab was the oldest among us and the entrepreneur of team. He made homemade desserts like cheesecakes from his cell and branded them with names like Coco Beyoncé. He sold the fragrance oils for the Muslim community so they could sustain themselves organizationally. Malik was a ballplayer from Brooklyn, a generation above me, also Muslim. Spud was a rapper and music producer and was a juvenile lifer. Shaq, another juvenile lifer, was the conscience of the group who would speak his mind with heartfelt impunity, but with a boyish tone. None of us were super cool with each other before this idea, but we came together for the creation of HOLLA.

A few weeks later, Malik was transferred to another prison. Shaq then recruited Arocks; and Arocks brought in Cory. Arocks was a free-spirited young brother who didn't know how *not* to smile, and he was a known Blood from Harlem. He shot someone in the stomach. Thankfully, the person was not seriously wounded. Arocks's father had been in prison since Arocks was a baby, so the substance of his entire relationship with his father was through prison visiting floors and letters. Cory, who I'd say was the nicest ballplayer of us all, was serving time for felony murder just like me. He was a Queens hard rock who rocked an afro with an afro pic. Cory and Arocks met each other in Rikers Island shortly after their arrest. They were fortunate enough to do most of their time together.

So here we were, a bunch of violent crooks meeting *while in prison* to build a program to save young people. Most criminal justice reforms leave people like us out of the policy proposals for decarceration. People like us are *too hard* to build enough public empathy. What these policy punks don't acknowledge is that prison is filled with humans who have the capacity to be just as brilliant as we can be dangerous—just like you. Opportunity tends to be the decision-maker for choosing brilliance.

After a couple of months we had created organizational bylaws and a curriculum, and we'd designed it all on the computer that I had access to in Transitional Services. We did the typing in the evening when we weren't so closely watched, because we could get into trouble for using the prison computers for personal use; and we were all willing to take that risk. No sense in having access if you are not using it in a way to benefit others.

Sadly, HOLLA never got off the ground while we were still in prison. We sent letters to people we knew in our communities outside, but we weren't taken seriously, or we were dismissed as being too risky because we were in prison. Despite it all, we kept meeting in the Blue Room, practicing presentations, and revising the curriculum. We had a full-on nonprofit organization in the works.

Two months after I came home, and was running HOLLA in a middle school in Brownsville, I took my first mentee to meet Eddie Ellis at his radio program, *On the Count*. That was the first time I met Eddie.

Throughout my years I had many Eddies traverse my life.

Another one of those Eddie Ellises was a woman who never served jail time. In 2007 Janis Rosheuvel was an organizer with an immigrant rights organization called Families for Freedom (FFF). Janis is Black and Guyanese, and she cussed like she did a shitload of prison time. She and her coworker Aarti Shahani, the former executive director of Families for Freedom, visited an organization that I was a part of in Otisville called Caribbean African Unity (CAU). Originally created by members of the original Green Haven Think Tank, including Eddie Ellis, in the mid-1980s, CAU was established to meet the specific needs of the African and Caribbean prison population. My boy Curtis, a Trinidadian older fella, started a chapter of CAU in Otisville. With his raspy Trini accent, he had said to me as we were leaving building 107, "Marlon, you have ah typewriter and yous Trini, so you goh be CAU secretary." I listened. To aid a group of men who were mostly facing deportation, we wrote letters to the consulates of the receiving countries and to NGOs seeking resources for the men and their families. Families for Freedom was one of the NGOs that responded to us.

CAU organized an event, a resource fair, where all the members of the prison organization could interact with a guest from outside, one of them being FFF. The resource fair was held in the gymnatorium—a basketball court that had a stage, which was the auditorium part. I was the host. My boy Huwe was the sound man with his keyboard. Yo, we were imagining our best Black lives. Janis and Aarti were super late, but we had to keep the event going. We had a set amount of time that we could be out of our housing units, so we organized a full program with speakers from other prison organizations to lead up to FFF. Because of their delay, I learned how to kill time on a stage with serious messaging and humor. I remember doing a little two-step to the instrumental of Jay-Z's "Show Me What You Got." Music could always make me feel free.

When Janis and Aarti arrived—they had gotten lost on the drive up—they spoke to an audience of uncertain Black men about what the landscape of immigration and deportation looked like from their end as organizers. It was bleak. Post-9/11 anxiety had released a ferocity of anti-immigrant rhetoric not seen since the Illegal Immigration Reform and Immigrant Responsibility Act of 1996. Under the guise of *reform*, the federal government expanded the offenses that could make an immigrant deportable. After 9/11, especially after the Patriot Act, even legal immigrants began getting deported at alarming rates.

Curtis and all the other founding members of the CAU were eventually deported. Prison offers no rewards for being selfless and contributing to humanity and community. Prison leeches time and dignity.

Janis and I promised to remain in contact, and we did. We cowrote an op-ed and I invited FFF back into the prison six months before my release for the first Reentry Resource Fair held at Otisville. Curtis and Andre, a leader in the Nation of Islam in Otisville, were the team of incarcerated men who organized the fair. After his release, Andre would become a close colleague and confidant of Eddie Ellis.

We organized the fair so that incarcerated men would present their solutions to the problem of parole board injustice, deportation, rehabilitation, and reentry. We had so much thought power behind those walls, and I was arrogant about showing that. I wanted us to feel seen.

Once Janis became the executive director of FFF, I asked her if I could volunteer with the organization when I was released.

"Yo ass better come fuck with us. Don't be saying you coming and then don't show up."

Janis believed in me. She saw me. Years later, as she was contemplating resignation, she asked me to apply to be the executive director. I applied, but I took my name out of the hat to start Youth Organizing to Save Our Streets, in my own Crown Heights neighborhood.

Like Nadia, Janis was another Black woman who led me to possibilities. Modern-day Harriet Tubmans, except they didn't have to brandish the rifle. I wanted my own gun to brandish with them. I wish I had learned earlier in life that there is utility in different types of guns.

CHAPTER TWELVE

PENS FROM THE PEN

In April 2008, Sean Bell's murderers, three New York City police officers who off-loaded fifty bullets at Bell and his friends after his bachelor party, were all acquitted of manslaughter. Michael Oliver, the detective who shot thirty-one rounds at Bell and his unarmed friends, said that the judge's not guilty decision (the defendants elected for a trial by judge) "was fair and just."[1] The morning of the decision I had arranged for all the TSC facilitators to watch the verdict live on television in building 107. Serious Black had warned me that I was about to be disappointed if I thought the police officers who had killed Bell would be held accountable by the court.

One month before that verdict, Senator Barack Obama had given an enthralling speech on race in America. It was called the "A More Perfect Union" speech. I had gotten my hands on the transcript of the senator's speech and dissected and highlighted phrases of the text like it was a school assignment. The hope and promise in his words were what made me feel that justice for Sean

Bell looked like criminal convictions of the shooters, and that there was no way that anything but a guilty verdict was certain.

Along with all the facilitators cramped around a twenty-inch television in a small classroom, I sat in silence as I heard the words "not guilty" repeated on the screen. One of the facilitators, Rocky, a forty-year-old Muslim, said, "What the fuck did you think was gonna happen, Marlon!" Serious Black smiled sarcastically. Another facilitator, Moses, packed up his belongings, a few books, and walked out of the room.

I should have known better, but I didn't. I was already locked up when the four officers who killed Amadou Diallo were acquitted of all charges. I witnessed COs bludgeon incarcerated men with impunity. Yet, yet, I still believed that a President Obama would change things. His "A More Perfect Union" speech gave me the hope he was selling.

The day after he gave his acceptance speech at the Democratic National Convention I wrote in my journal:

> Obama has changed our culture. Usually at 11:00 am when I get back to the dorm from program the guys are watching 106th & Park or a movie. Today I walked into the dayroom to see CSPAN on the tv. Congresspeople were debating the $700 billion bailout plan. This past Friday we watched the presidential debate. Whether Obama wins or not he has already shifted the perpetual political ignorance of Blacks and other minorities to political astuteness. He has changed American culture.

The night he gave his acceptance speech after winning the presidency I was the last person in the dayroom. That night I wrote:

Tonight I cried.

President Barack H. Obama.

So many emotions. To be a Black man with a troubled past. A Black man that sees color, but doesn't dwell on it. The whips, chains, lynchings, nigger this & nigger that, crack buildings, you gotta work twice as hard as a white person, the struggle, hopes, Jehovah I don't know what I feel, but I know that I am proud. I feel like we-we-we have won something. I am happy that my knowledge of my history enables me to understand the significance of this historic day.

Later that same year, on December 27, I gave a speech for the annual Kwanzaa celebration that the prison's African American Organization organized every December. Different guys were asked to give a speech for every evening of Kwanzaa for the twenty to forty people who came to listen in a small room above the gymnatorium. Two months after Obama's election I honored that feat on the night of Kujichagulia, the second principle of Kwanzaa, which represented self-determination. I began the speech with:

As a fledgling journalist and someone who takes pride in being in tune with current events I am a bit ashamed that I cannot recall when I first heard his name. Embarrassed that when I did hear his name and of his ambitions that I didn't take him seriously—laughed him off as an afterthought, didn't bother memorizing his name or listening to him speak; didn't consider his thoughts, his story, HIS DEFINITION OF HIMSELF.

I think the first time I paid any attention to him on the television or gave a listening ear to the conversation about him was on 98.7 KISS FM's Open Line radio talk show in early March.

Then came the slew of categorizations:

He was an African, Hawaiian, a Kenyan, a Muslim, a Christian, a black not black enough, too black, an idealist, a good speaker, another Jesse, another Al, too passive, a coke sniffer, an opportunist, a spoiler, a Sambo that whites were comfortable with, an uppity Negro, an elitist, a socialist, too nice, easygoing, too intelligent, not experienced enough, over his head, too young, out of his mind, a racist...

The definitions attributed to this man were given by Blacks, Whites, Latinos, Asians; by the poor, by the rich, by the free, by the incarcerated.

The questions that would remain were:

Would he accept the definitions given to him? Would he buckle under the pressure to fit into the categories that people—which we—wanted him to fit into?

No.

On that defining moment on November fourth this man defined himself. Through his self-determination he defined himself, simultaneously initiating the redefinition of this country; the redefinition of how we view ourselves in this country. There is a Black CO in this prison that is pregnant; we all know her. Irrespective of what you think about her, we must acknowledge that her unborn son or daughter will be born into a world where the sight of a Black person in the highest office in this country will not be a shock, it will be a matter of fact. Unlike us who see his election as an event that we thought we would never see, this child will not have any limitation to his or her imagination or reality.

His self-determination inspired so many of us to watch CNN, MSNBC, and FOX News. He inspired us to read more than the sports section of the newspapers. His self-determination inspired us, the most marginalized and politically blasphemed of society, to talk in this prison, debating about things we never thought about before: left wing and right wing politics, pork barrels, the electoral college, senate seats, bipartisan politics, and so on.

His self-determination for self-definition inspired and proved that the young, the hip hop and dance hall generation, the iPOD and MP3 kids, and the BET and MTV fans were more than what mainstream media and out-of-touch older Blacks and Latinos thought of us.

His self-determination to be self-defined inspired Blacks and Latinos, old and young, West Indians and African Americans, Latin Kings and Netas, Bloods and Crips to watch the television in their day rooms and listen to their Walkmans and Super 3 radios as he gave his victory speech saying:

"This is our moment, this is our time.... In this new world, success will mean the active pursuit of excellence, not the passive avoidance of failure."

After the Kwanzaa speech, I organized the men to write their hopes for Obama's presidency, which I mailed to the White House and *Essence* magazine.

Oscar Grant III, an unarmed Black man, was killed in Oakland, California, by BART police four days after I gave this speech of hope.

Prison can do this thing where the prisoner becomes more invested in the binary of right versus wrong than the most conservative prosecutor. Guilt does that. Living with the memory that you were the purveyor of some great harm toward another person or people can have the unintended effect of blinding you to the injustice of being treated unfairly. Critiquing a system for injury can feel sacrilegious and incongruent with accepting guilt for your personal transgressions. Obama represented for me, in the last year of my bid, possibility, which I already aligned with, but he also reinforced for me the idea that all I had to do was be a good citizen and everything was gonna be alright. Stay away from guns, old habits, and old friends, and life after prison would be much easier. I spewed lots of that rhetoric in the classes I conducted inside.

What Obama's race speech left out was that no amount of goodness on the parts of Black people would prevent us from filling up American jails, prisons, immigration lockups, and special housing units within those jails, prisons, and lockups. Obama's speech on race left out the American fact that this process of building toward a more perfect union is accomplished on the backs of dead Black people who were involuntarily sacrificed to ideals of life, liberty, and the pursuit of happiness.

Years later I found myself being a huge critic of President Obama, not because he wasn't a good man or a great leader, but because he was not being real enough with us. It is not our job as Black people to make this nation more perfect. It's our responsibility to heal; to create Black joy; to realize a world of Black possibilities—not to be the bastard laborers of an American perfection that relies on our involuntary martyrdom.

There are parts of that 2008 speech that I no longer align myself with. There are essays and journal entries from that time I no longer agree with. I was becoming freer from the guilt of my transgressions. I was in the process of becoming whole. The part of that speech I still retain as personal creed are the words I recited by Dr. Joy DeGruy, author of *Post Traumatic Slavery Syndrome*. I closed that Kwanzaa speech with this:

Put these in your mental rolodexes:

1) Are you destroying or creating?

2) Have you discovered your unique gift and shared it with others?

3) Do things get worse or do they improve around you?

4) Are others' lives poorer or richer because you are alive?

5) Do you make the world a better place? (The world is your surroundings—your family, your friends, and so on)

6) When people leave your company do they feel better than before you arrived?

—Define ourselves

—Create for ourselves, and

—Speak for ourselves

Instead of being defined, named, created for, or spoken for by others.

Our family, community, and culture depend on it.

I was woke and ready to leave this prison.

CHAPTER THIRTEEN

UN-AMERICAN AND FREE

Fuck prison.

Seven days before I was released my sleeping area was ransacked by COs in search of something, I am still unsure what. A former Bridging the Gap participant, a Vassar student, sent me a Vassar-lettered hoodie as a gift to wear home. It was December, so warm clothes made sense. The hoodie triggered the prison administration's suspicion that I was having inappropriate relationships with the Vassar students and that I was getting favors from them. Sargent Shayborn had his officers confiscate every letter, picture, and journal entry I had in my sleeping area. They left my remaining clothes and books alone. They wanted to invade the most intimate parts of me—the sacred layers. After several days of reading letters sent to me and journal entries from the decade of my twenties, a CO, a chubby thirty-something-year-old white man named Conklin, who always wore his dingy DOCCS baseball cap, returned my belongings and jeeringly said, "Peterson, you gave a fuck. You really did give a fuck, but why didn't you write about me?" People like this officer are why I take a personal affront to law enforcement when they speak to me as if I am a toy to be played with. They had all the evidence to prove that their suspicions were wrong, but they didn't care about evidence. They had a preconceived notion about people like me that no amount of evidence could disprove. Six days before my freedom date, Sargent Shayborn had me escorted to his office where he told me, "The Lord must be on your side because if you had a little more time left, I would lose you in the system."

Fuck him, and his belief in my worst possibilities, despite my living a life inside where people kept instilling hope in me. He wanted to keep me in prison based on an idea he had in his head. He wanted to keep me away from my father, mother, sister, brother, and nephew for *an idea he had in his head*. Prison didn't want to let me go.

A couple of hours before my release I wrote my final journal entry from prison:

So, it's 2 am and in 6–7 hours I'll be out of prison. Am I ready? Absolutely. Nervous? Absolutely not. Devon, Mike, & Kels are coming to pick me up. This part of my life is over…

…and the next stage begins.

Jehovah God thank you. I did not become the stereotyped person in prison. No fights. No beefs. No drugs. No gangs. Smarter, wiser, more secure. A better man. Stronger fam ties. Better friends.

I've conquered prison! I will be successful. I will break barriers. I will inspire. I will because it is what I ought to do.

And 2 Corinthians 4:16–18. G-YEA! My sabbatical is finished. My new life begins. Stay tuned.

[Peace and love to the people harmed by our collective act
of violence in 1999]
10/13/99–12/23/09

December 23, 2009, was the most anticlimactic day of my entire 3,722 days in prison. Nothing felt different to me. The CO
covering my housing unit asked why I didn't seem excited about
going home. I don't remember my answer, but I do recall won-
dering, "How should I be acting right now?" I was nineteen years
old when I went away. My freedom would forever be connected
to the death of innocent people. I knew I'd always be considered
an ex-con. How many times would I have to prove to people that
I was no longer that nineteen-year-old boy? Would I be wrong if
part of me had wanted to experience my nineteenth, twentieth,
twenty-first, twenty-second, twenty-third, twenty-fourth, twenty-
fifth, twenty-sixth, twenty-seventh, twenty-eighth, twenty-ninth,
and thirtieth birthday out of prison? Did I deserve to imagine
freedom? The four people shot, the two who died, the neighborhood that was traumatized by the shooting—they all suffer, still.

Sometimes I get a horrid taste in my mouth when I hear people
spew about "mass incarceration," "mass deportation," and "criminal
justice reform." Everyone likes to quote Bryan Stevenson's "I believe
that each person is more than the worst thing they've ever done,"
but no one ever thinks about how difficult it is for the person who
committed the wrong to believe that they aren't forever wrong. I
imagined the impact of my decisions on the people who were sitting
in that restaurant; the people who were running in the streets when
the shooting happened; the mothers who lost their sons that day; the
immigrant worker who probably didn't have good enough health in-
surance to fully pay for their healing. I know I didn't shoot anyone,

but I remember wanting to have a gun with me that day. Why was I so broken that I could volunteer to carry a deadly weapon to a robbery? I had never shot anyone, so why was I so eager to be in a position to shoot someone? Someone I had never seen, or knew existed?

In the years that followed my release, I implemented HOLLA in two schools in Brooklyn, worked as a violence interrupter in my own Crown Heights neighborhood; mentored and spoke to thousands of kids like myself from Brooklyn to Durban, South Africa; published essays in some amazing publications; gave a TED talk that amassed over one million views; and helped get my boy Khalil Cumberbatch out of immigration detention. I have loads of awards from organizations and politicians for my work in my community. I got a degree from New York University. People send me emails and direct messages on Instagram, Facebook, and Twitter to tell me how much they have been inspired by some aspect of my work. I got receipts, and for all of this I am in deep gratitude. When I travel to other countries, I insert time to bask in the blessings that I have been bestowed.

But the prison that I have had the hardest time identifying and abolishing is the one that has convinced me that I do not deserve to be happy; that happiness is a fleeting moment, but never a movement. I guess that's why my smiling in pictures is revolutionary. The opponent is every horrible experience I've had. Every lie that I've believed in, and every one I have told lugs along as though it's attached to my ankle like a ball and chain. Lies have been my most despotic captor.

Even in this book I have lied. Until now I omitted that at eighteen I beat and hung a dog and came close to shooting it while it was crying. I conveniently left out that I have never been faithful or entirely truthful to any woman who has loved or lusted for me. I was the good guy fukboy. I was actively a piece of shit to others. As much as I needed to be seen as fully human, I was denying the women in my life that same humanity: to be seen as more than an object with which I could be selfish about comfort, and comfortable with being at my worst. About lying. The footnote nature of this admission is proof that I've struggled with the comfort of the victim role.

I daydream about my death as an event when I will get to hear people speak about the way I have positively impacted their lives. That's some narcissistic shit. Nothing is balanced out here. It's not excusable for a victim to become a perpetrator, or for the perpetrator to claim victimhood. But they are realities. These polarities exist in every moment.

I didn't tell you that Marlon is still scared and uncomfortable with smiling in pictures. I've wanted not to exist more times than I've wanted to live, and no child should ever think about invisibility as a way out of the day. Neither should any adult. I never attempted suicide, but I thought about it a lot, and sometimes I still think about it. This is what prison feels like. Trapped. I think about death from the police, death from somebody in the street, and sometimes by an accident. I am a Black person in America, so this ain't only me. I wanted to write it out because I want to heal.

I want to end all the prisons that bind us.

We need to abolish lies—the ones we tell and the ones we are told. Our imaginations can become a reality only when we are freer and more honest.

There are 2.3 million people in actual prisons in America, almost 400,000 locked in Immigration and Customs Enforcement detention centers, over 70 million people living in the US with a criminal conviction, over 4.5 million under some form of state supervision, including e-carceration. Yo, we digitizing incarceration. What does this say about a society that basks in the peace of captivity?

America is an incarcerated republic, and I have told you before that I do not like prisons of any kind. This is why I aim to be a better un-American. For so long I have hidden pain, consciously hurt others, and survived in the deceit of it all. That's what we men do. This is how we define manhood. Phrases like "men don't cry," "men don't show emotion," and "men are tough" promote unevolved customs, and they are still embedded in the ethos of America. I don't think of America in a gendered binary. I experience this nation as a charismatic brute of a man. American patriotism is American patriarchy, and I don't want to pledge any allegiance to that. I don't want to keep that kind of company anymore.

America, he hurts people all over the world every day—and I mean "he" because our warped performance of malignant masculinity is what makes America so great in the eyes of the world. Not every country was created by war and the written oppression of most of its citizens; not every country in the world gained its wealth through the brazen brutality of slavery, war, colonialism, and dogged capitalism. Therein lies the ethos of American exceptionalism. But just like me, America is enveloped in emotional deadness, apathetic to the hurt it is causing in plain sight. America is a cauldron of weakness that harms Black people, immigrants, and women to protect itself from the foibles of its foundation. A foundation built on an ideal of white supremacy that has no real grounding. White supremacy is fake as fuck, but it feels so good. The details are in the deception.

I was being an American. I was complicit in the idea of white supremacy, an idea that white people incarnate, but is not exclusive to white skin. The idea that difference is threatening to personal existence; that pain can be forgotten without being acknowledged; that personal freedom can exist without a collective honesty and commitment to healing. In so many ways I am still an American.

I am most fittingly an unproud-unAmerican-American. I understand the privileges American citizenship affords me. I get to not be harassed by law enforcement. Lie. I get to not be marginalized because of my skin color. Lie. I get to access the best public school education in the world. Lie.[1] I get to live in a country that is free of domestic terrorism. Lie.[2] I get to live in the best democracy in the world. Another lie. I get to live in a country where the electoral process is fair and uncorrupted. Hold up, that's not right because of gerrymandering, voter suppression, and that stolen election thing that happened back in 2000 when Al Gore won, but Bush Jr. got the court, not the electorate, to crown him king.

So, yes, I am an unproud-unAmerican-American. I don't pledge allegiance to people that won't do the same for me. Why would I act differently for a nation that doesn't love me or the people I care about?

Everything about this ungreatful (sic) nation is worth being (un) proud about. White immigrants bravely fleeing persecution to begin again in a new land and being deified for being brave; Black Caribbean and Latin American immigrants bravely seeking new beginnings and opportunities and being ostracized for being brave. Proud then unproud. Welcoming immigrants to (un) welcoming immigrants.

Men creating a nation ebbed in freedom for all. Men creating a nation of unprecedented freedoms—except for everyone not white and male. A nation premised on liberty for all. A nation that consciously and conscientiously applies this notion of liberty on the foundations of slavery, convict lease gangs, mass incarceration, and now, deportation. Proud then unproud.

America the beautiful founded on masculinity and grit. America the scoffed beacon that has more guns than people, and more gun deaths than any other first world nation (whatever that is). America the blighted that loves the brutal bravery of its beginning more than its ideals of justice for all. Proud then unproud.

America the indivisible that saw hope and fortune for itself in its manifest destiny. America the nation that saw ghettoes—that created ghettos as the destiny for the descendants of slaves and immigrants. America that saw no one other than itself. Proud then unproud.

America is me—a lie that supports its original injustice. Being dishonest with self.

Yet Black people like me can never be fully American in all of his sordid delusions. American freedom codifies that white people can be as free and rebellious as they want to be—with or without a cause. Only the America of white people could so cavalierly parade, lallygag, and chase government officials from their place of work—the center of the American Republic, the US Capitol. Black people like me will never feel so American that we would instigate or perform a coup d'état without first accepting that such an act is a death wish. We calculate our risks. We believe that Black Lives Matter more than Americanism.

My first seven days of jail were the most dizzying days of my life. The shock of cuffs, cells, judges, COs, and danger everywhere made me feel uncertain and helpless. I dreamt I was awake, and when I was awake my mind would sleep. I rarely used the bathroom that week. I ate nothing. I didn't know how to use the phone. I was afraid to shower because of the prison stories people always joked about. I was in a lineup. I had no heat in my cell. I didn't have toothpaste. I didn't have a change of clothes.

And then, I adjusted. The chaos didn't stop, but my relationship to it changed. I wanted to beat prison, so I started asking questions of myself, then the system: "Why are you the way you are?" and "Why won't you do anything about it?"

I've told you why I am the way I am, and the way I was. This story about this uncaged bird—me—being freer than I was yesterday. Unshackled. Cut. Scabbed. Healing. Scab again. Heal again.

Healing is my process for abolishing prisons. Healing can win when we commit to truth-telling. There is no real way to hide from the truth, only ways to lie to yourself. Prisons shackle, cut, and scab. Scabs win when we invest in prisons. So I prefer to create melodies of freedom through words, through actions of inspiration—bop my head to them. I play steelpan again in the summers. The melodies of the six-bass dancing in unison with the other pans still give me peace of mind. Today I am better than I was yesterday. My experiences have taught me that there is nothing prettier and more soothing than freedom, and that there are lessons, not baggage, to be gained from my Dash.

The first time I decided that Dash would be your name I was in my mid-thirties at a funeral for a nineteen-year-old boy who was shot to death—the same age I was when I went to prison. I feel better now, and sometimes I don't.

Tell me about your Dash, be free, and please remember this before you speak…

I do not believe in prisons of any kind. I believe in freedom, and that is who I write to today.

Dear Freedom,

You are elusive, priceless, and beautiful. You are ornamented with kente stitching and adorned with colorful beads. Your smile is radiant and your presence is a priceless present. Freedom, you are the one thing that I was once afraid to accept because somewhere along the course of my life I believed I was undeserving of you. That is why I spoke so much about being in chains. I felt more comfortable sitting in a bed of bondage. It was a more sensational identity. Prisons are more appealing than freedom. That is why there are dozens more television shows that highlight lockups than there are programs that showcase the levels of freedom that are not attached to wealth and social status. But that isn't me—not anymore—I hope.

Freedom, I value the deep process of loving you because you are not perfect. So I will talk and write more about the attainment of you and less about what we don't want, which are prisons that we create and those that are created for us. I've realized that I don't need to tell the world about the prisons we already know exist. I will write more about the ways to appreciate the journey to freedom; the strategies to freedom obtainment; and the pricelessness and beauty of accepting freedom.

I can feel you waiting with open arms for my liberated spirit now that my journey of return has been accomplished.

There is nothing more powerful than a human who understands who they really are. We all deserve to live in a world without prisons. We deserve more than a prison identity.

I am uncaged and I identify with you.

Happiness is next.

In peace,

Marlon

ACKNOWLEDGMENTS

I needed to write this book. For you, Marlo'. You needed these words more than anyone else. If no one but you receives these words, I will feel accomplished, so, to you Marlo', the younger me, thank you for surviving despite it all. I wrote this book for you, and because of you.

Versions of this book have been in my head since I was about twenty-five, and in the fifteen years that it took for me to complete it I have so many people to thank for keeping me going, pushing me, and seeing possibilities for me that cages blinded from my sights.

Elsa Peterson and Michael Peterson, my parents, I don't have to hope that I've made you proud of me. Thank you for showing me that I mattered to you even during those years of prison, when it hurt you to see me hate myself. Daddy, you did a great job, and not even dementia can erase your love away from me, and my affection for you. Mommy, my twin, thank you for being more than my mother—for being Elsa. I love soca music and whining because of you. Kelly, Mikey, and Devon, you all have been my anchors. I know you all cried for me, and because of me, and this book is an offering to you all as well. I don't know how I would have remained sane all those years without knowing you all were in my corner. But, especially you, Dev, I thank you for Jen, Logie, and Leo. Like always, you inspire me to smile just because you are alive. Me & You, we did it! So much love to my reentry program of extended family members: Tasha, Tony, Pauline, Les-Marie, Wesley, Aunty Sharon, Lisa, Camille, Uncle Roy, Nesha, Romel, Nicholas, Mark, Aunty Lorna, Aunty Judy, Ricky, Kurt, Michelle, Osa, and David "Ben-Eye." To Dwayne Sargent and Terrell Tate, you two have rode this rollercoaster with me since childhood. Dwayne, thank you for the three-way calls, and for always keeping me grounded. Terrell, you have always been the good angel trying to prevent me from Marloning up things. Joseph Crossland, nothing can break our bond.

Dr. Nadia Lopéz, you breathed life into my soul, and for that you will always be my sister from another mister. Crown Heights, Bed-Stuy, Brownsville, and Flatbush, we did it!

Darnell L. Moore and Kiese Laymon, you two have encouraged and cared for me since we met. I know it took crazy long to finish this book (don't clown me), but y'all made a bruh feel like a real writer. Because of you I met my agent Katie Kotchman and editors Katy O'Donnell and Claire Zuo. But, more important, you two brothers, who write to live, have taught me the value of Black men loving each other without boundaries.

To Lu Chen, my HOLLA brothers: Clifton "Bill" Hall, Cory Greene, Arocks, Butta Lab, Shaq; to El Sun, Divine, Huwe "Wise" Burton, Richard Mayo, Charzell McGill, Gaspari Bernardin, Dâvey Shark, Milas Ringer, Gary Johnson, Gavin Bourne, Brother Carter, Benjamin Grimes, Mike Vega, Calvin M., Dennis DeRose, Boo, Carlton Ficklin, Big John, Spank, Ms. Paris, Donna Hylton, Curtis Houlder (CAU), "X" Nelson, Tracie

Moore, Akilah Charles, Natasha Cossiah, Curtis Archer, y'all took good care of me while I was inside.

To all the Bridging the Gap Vassar students who became my friends: Kleaver Cruz, Willa Conway, Erica Licht, Oscar Prado, Ryan Greenlee, Jon Turner, Hensleigh Crowell, Smiling Sara, Stephanie Damon-Moore, Sarah Fairchild, Victor Monterrosa Jr., Stephanie Buntin, Illana Yamin, Eva Grenier, and more, I hope you learned as much from me as I did from you.

Mychal Denzel Smith, brother, I love your words. Wade Davis, you pave ways, man, thank you. To the rest of my Brothers Writing to Live family, kai m. green, Nyle Fort, Mark Anthony Neal, I still can't believe that I get to be in your company.

Ife Charles, you can feel when I need to be pulled out of self-doubt and depression. You are my spiritual guide. Ruby-Beth Buitekant, thank you for showing me that it is okay to celebrate my birthday...with french fries. I don't think Youth Organizing to Save Our Streets would have worked without you. Brittney Cooper, your words during that Black Brilliance Brunch probably prevented me from walking off of a train track. To Kimberlie Crenshaw, Luke Harris, Priscilla Ocen, Devon Carbado, Paul Butler, Laura Flanders, Alvin Starks, and Andrea Ritchie, your brilliance intimidated me, and gave me something to aspire to. Janis Rosheuvel, thanks for introducing me to organizing. Dawn Shedrick, you saw me and stood for me from the arc.

Big ups to my comrades Baz Dreisinger, Stephanie Weekes, Malik Yoba, Phillip Edwards, Merv, Mega, Bre Scullark, TL Lewis, Daniella Nuñez, Elayne Fluker, Hernan Carventé, Glenn E. Martin, Topeka K. Sam, Shaka Senghor, Kirk James, Mary Hooks, Rukia Lumumba, Noel Didla, Richard Wallace, Trevaughn Hall, Opal Tometti, Alicia Garza, Fatima Ashraf, Sheila

Rule, Rob Gore, Chanda Prescod-Weinstein, Phyllis Kemi Senah, Andre Richardson, Wayne McKenzie, Shaka Mentor, Leah Marville, Sophia Chang, Vicky Moriarty, and Natasha Gaspard. Kerry Keith and Nicole Alexander, you two helped me become a more organized visionary; to my Atlantic Fellows for Racial Equity family, (Black&)TED fam, Aspen family, especially AfroAspen, the world is ours to love and create anew. Nike Irvin, you are amazing. To my NYC gun violence prevention fam, Derrick Scott, Pana, Amy Ellenbogen, Chiz, Rudy Suggs, AT Mitchell, Erica Ford, Shanduke McPhatter, Monique Chandler-Waterman, K. Bain, Iesha Sekou, Jumaane Williams, Shaina Harrison, Rebecca Fischer, Anthony Newerls, you all have saved so many lives. Thanks for showing me the ropes, Chicago Cure Violence fam and Families for Freedom.

To the Trinidad and Tobago communities of Laventille, Sea Lots, Beetham Gardens, Point Fortin, St. James, and the first part of Trinidad I called home, Queens Street and Nelson Street, I see you, will always knock ah pan for alyuh. Mtima Solwazi, thanks for showing me around. To the family in Hanover Park, Cape Town, South Africa, I see you—Amandla.

To the people trapped in cages created for you, I see you.

Akaijah Evelyn and Lavon Walker, you two were taken away too soon.

If I forgot to mention you, blame the weed, not my heart.

NOTES

Chapter 1. Hiding

1. History staff, "U.S. Immigration Since 1965," History, updated June 7, 2019, https://www.history.com/topics/immigration/us-immigration-since-1965.

2. Jennifer Ludden, "1965 Immigration Law Changed Face of America," NPR, May 9, 2006, https://www.npr.org/templates/story/story.php?storyId=5391395.

Chapter 2. Move On

1. Joseph B. Treaster, "Brooklyn Businessman Strangled in a Struggle with Police Officers," *The New York Times*, June 17, 1978, https://www.nytimes.com/1978/06/17/archives/brooklyn-businessman-strangled-in-a-struggle-with-police-officers-2.html.

2. "1995 Report to the Congress: Cocaine and Federal Sentencing Policy," United States Sentencing Commission, https://www.ussc.gov/research/congressional-reports/1995-report-congress-cocaine-and-federal-sentencing-policy.

3. Eliza Shapiro, "Only 7 Black Students Got Into Stuyvesant, N.Y.'s Most Selective High School, Out of 895 Spots," *The New York Times*, March 19, 2019, https://www.nytimes.com/2019/03/18/nyregion/black-students-nyc-high-schools.html.

Chapter 5. Okay

1. "Mass Shootings in America," Stanford Libraries, 2012, https://library.stanford.edu/projects/mass-shootings-america.

2. Pantonic Steel Orchestra—1999 New York Panorama—In My House, WSTglobalHD, YouTube video, October 1, 2013, https://www.youtube.com/watch?v=7nHdWPxoqHI.

Chapter 10. Bridging the Gap

1. Kassandra I. Alcaraz, Katherine S. Eddens, Jennifer L. Blase, W. Ryan Diver, Alpa V. Patel, Lauren R. Teras, Victoria L. Stevens, Eric J. Jacobs, Susan M. Gapstur, "Social Isolation and Mortality in US Black and White Men and Women," *American Journal of Epidemiology*, Volume 188, Issue 1 (January 2019), 102–109, https://doi.org/10.1093/aje/kwy231.

2. Allen J. Beck, Ramona R. Rantala, and Jessica Rexroat, "Sexual Victimization Reported by Adult Correctional Authorities, 2009–11." U.S. Department of Justice, Office of Justice Programs, Bureau of Justice Statistics, January 2014, https://www.bjs.gov/content/pub/pdf/svraca0911.pdf.

3. "From Criminal Justice to Human Justice," The Center for NuLeadership on Human Justice & Healing, n.d., https://www.nuleadership.org/#raising-funds.

Chapter 12. Pens from the Pen

1. Michael Wilson, "3 Detectives Acquitted in Bell Shooting," *The New York Times*, April 26, 2008, https://www.nytimes.com/2008/04/26/nyregion/26BELL.html.

Chapter 13. Un-American and Free

1. Julia Ryan, "American Schools vs. the World: Expensive, Unequal, Bad at Math," *The Atlantic*, December 3, 2013, https://www.theatlantic.com/education/archive/2013/12/american-schools-vs-the-world-expensive-unequal-bad-at-math/281983/.

2. Arie Perliger, "Homegrown Terrorism and Why the Threat of Right-Wing Extremism Is Rising in America," *Newsweek*, June 4, 2017, https://www.newsweek.com/homegrown-terrorism-rising-threat-right-wing-extremism-619724.

Marlon Peterson is the principal of The Precedential Group Social Enterprises, a social good impact firm. He is host of the *Decarcerated Podcast*, a Senior Atlantic Institute Fellow for Racial Equity, a Civil Society Fellow of the Aspen Global Leadership Network, and a 2015 recipient of the Soros Justice Fellowship. *Ebony* magazine has named him one of America's 100 most influential and inspiring leaders in the Black community. His TED talk, "Am I Not Human? A Call for Criminal Justice Reform," has over 1.2 million views. He contributed to Kiese Laymon's book *How to Slowly Kill Yourself and Others in America* and Akiba Solomon and Kenrya Rankin's *How We Fight White Supremacy*. His writing has appeared in *Ebony, The Nation, USA Today, Colorlines*, and more. A graduate of New York University, he lives in Brooklyn and plays the steelpan during the summer.